UNDER THE EAVES OF ARCHITECTURE THE AGA KHAN: BUILDER AND PATRON

Philip Jodidio

PRESTEL Munich | Berlin | London | New York

CONTENTS

BUILDER
OF BRIDGES

This book is not about architecture. It is about a man and his commitment to bettering the life of many through improvements to the physical environment. Architecture, after all, not as a goal in and of itself, but as an integral part of the "processes of change" required to give dignity, comfort, education and hope to thousands. Not just buildings, but places to live, worship, study and work. Not the modernity of the *tabula rasa*, but one of measured, appropriate development that does not reject tradition. How can one man have an appreciable impact on the vast questions raised by the physical environment of a quarter of humanity? How can an individual create a bridge between the *umma*,[1] or the "Community of Believers", and those of other faiths, so that mutual understanding, indeed pluralism, can advance against the tides of doubt and prejudice? The answer to this question lies partly in history that goes back to the sixth century.

A brief description of the Muslim faith may well serve as an introduction to some of the issues raised by the involvement of His Highness the Aga Khan in architecture: "Muslims are those who submit to God. They are a community of the middle path, of balance, which is taught to avoid extremes, to enjoin good and forbid evil, using the best of arguments. Such a community eschews compulsion, leaves each to their own faith and encourages all to vie for goodness: it is the nobility of conduct that endears one in the sight of God. In its pristine sense, Islam refers to the inner struggle of the individual, waged singly and in consonance with fellow believers, to engage in earthly life, and yet, to rise above its trappings in search of the Divine. But that quest is only meaningful in tandem with the effort to do good for the kin, the orphan, the needy, the vulnerable; to be just, honest, humble, tolerant and forgiving."[2] The Aga Khan has again and again, through his institutions, his speeches and his personal involvement, underlined the importance of architecture as an integral part of the physical environment. To improve the quality of life in the Muslim world, he has sought not only to build, but, perhaps more importantly, to seek a way to build, so that tradition and modernity can be reconciled, so that the past can find its rightful place in the present and the future. The question of how tradition relates to modernity is, of course, central to contemporary architecture, considered from the Western and professional point of view. The Aga Khan approaches this issue from a different direction, related to his role as a Muslim religious leader, and as a man educated in the West. The point lies precisely in not giving a prize to a glittering new building that speaks of surface and acknowledges no past, but in searching for the inner meaning, the essence of architecture, be it religious or secular. His goal is also, undoubtedly, quite simply to bring people together so that they may speak and understand each other, to build bridges between worlds.

The Presence of the Past

The Shia Imami Ismaili Muslims, usually known as Ismailis, belong to the Shia branch of Islam. Roughly fifteen million Ismailis live in more than twenty-five countries, mainly in Asia, Africa and the Middle East, as well as in Europe, Canada and the United States. Despite this geographic dispersion, they form a well-organized community. In common with other Shia Mus-

Above, the mosque /
madrasa of Umm
al-Sultan Shaaban
in the Darb al-Ahmar
district of Cairo,
Egypt, near Azhar
Park.

Left, a gouache by the
Egyptian architect
Hassan Fathy of the
Hamdi Seif al-Nasr
house, *c.* 1937.

lims, Ismailis affirm that after the Prophet's death in 632, Hazrat Ali, the Prophet's cousin and son-in-law, became the first Imam – the spiritual leader of the Muslim community – and that this spiritual leadership, known as the Imamat, continues thereafter by heredity through Ali and his wife, Fatima, the Prophet's daughter. Succession to the Imamat, according to Shia doctrine and tradition, is by way of *nass* (designation), and it is the absolute preroga-tive of the Imam to appoint his successor. Ismailis derive their name from their allegiance to Ismail Ibn Jafar (721–755), the eldest son of the Shia Imam Ja-far al-Sadiq (702–765). The Imamat is one of the underlying principles of Shia Islam: "The Imam being the spiritual guide, and in view of the importance that Islam places on maintaining a balance between the material and spiritual well-being of Muslims, the Imam's guidance must deal with both aspects of the life of his community."[3] His Highness Prince Karim Aga Khan is thus the forty-ninth hereditary Imam of the Shia Imami Ismaili Muslims, in direct lineal de-scent from Prophet Mohammed through Ali and Fatima. He succeeded his grandfather, Sir Sultan Mahomed Shah Aga Khan, to the Imamat on 11 July 1957 at the age of twenty.

Ismailis have long contributed to the advancement of science, math-ematics and, indeed, architecture. In the tenth century, an Ismaili Imam, Ubayd Allah al-Mahdi Billah, founded the Fatimid state in Tunisia (named after Fatima, the Prophet's daughter from whom the Fatimid Imam/Caliphs traced their an-cestry). His successors spread the first significant Shia state to areas of North Africa, including Egypt and parts of Arabia. It was during this Fatimid Caliphate (909–1171) that the early contributions of Ismailis reached their height, with the founding of Cairo,[4] and the building in that city of al-Azhar Mosque (969–971), together with its school of theology or *madrasa* (988). The full name of the Prophet was Sayeda Fatima al-Zahra', whence the name of the mosque (meaning "the most flourishing and shining" in Arabic). Dar al-'Ilm, or the "House of Knowledge", was established in Cairo in 1005 by al-Hakim bi-Amr Allah, the sixth Fatimid Imam/Caliph. Dar al-'Ilm was nothing less than the first medieval institution of higher learning and thus a precursor of modern universities. Studies there in-cluded a full range of the academic disciplines, from religion to jurisprudence, grammar, medicine, logic, mathematics and astronomy. Significantly, the institution was open to followers of different religions. The Fatimids were noted for their wide-ranging trade with areas as far distant as southern Italy and Corsica to Asia, and also because government officers were appointed on reasons of merit rather than on the basis of heredity. Sunnis, and even Christians or Jews, thus occupied high positions under the Caliphate. The Fatimids also encouraged the practice of private patronage of mosques and other religious buildings by Muslims of different persuasions. The Muslim doctrine of justice and equality thus put into practice is an essential aspect of the faith and action of Ismailis, in particular as expressed through the voice of the Imam. When the Aga Khan speaks today of pluralism and acts to defend it, he is upholding a thousand-year-old tradition. When he creates a university, as he has in Karachi and is now doing in Central Asia, the Aga Khan is also walking in the footsteps of his ancestors even as he looks to the future.

At the end of the eleventh century, a schism led part of the Ismaili community to vow its alle-giance to the eldest son of the Imam/Caliph Ma'd Abu Tamim, called al-Mustansir Billah. The present Aga Khan traces his ancestry from Imam Nizar, whose followers established themselves in Alamut, in northern Iran, and later in parts of Syria. The Mongol horde of Mongke Khan vanquished this second Ismaili state in 1256, and many of its people found refuge in Afghanistan, Central Asia, China, or India, while others remained in Syria. Although the Fatimids had already spread through many countries, it was this cataclysm that in a sense signed the destiny of the Ismailis, people of a diaspora who remained faithful to their beliefs and to their Imam.

His Highness the Aga Khan

The Ismaili community entered its modern phase when Aga Hasan Ali Shah (1800–81), given the title Aga Khan I by the Emperor of Persia Fat' h Ali Shah Qajar, established himself in Bombay (now Mumbai) in 1848. The name Aga Khan derives from the Turkish military title 'Agha' combined with the Turkic, Mongolian or Persian/Pashto title 'Khan', thus translating into numerous languages as "Commanding Chief". Forty-sixth Imam of the Ismailis, Aga Khan I had been Governor General of the Persian province of Kerman before a dispute with the Shah led him to seek the protection of the British in India. This accident of history led to increased contact between the far-flung community and the Imam, and also to the British granting him the title 'His Highness'. He was succeeded by his eldest son Aga Khan II, who died in 1885 just four years after becoming Imam.

At the age of eight, Sultan Mahomed Shah became Aga Khan III, receiving the title 'His Highness' from Queen Victoria the following year in 1886. Born in Karachi, he was one of the founders and first President of the All-India Muslim League and President of the League of Nations (1937–38). Above all, Aga Khan III created numerous institutions for social and economic development on the Indian subcontinent and in East Africa. In many ways, the significance and breadth of these initiatives laid the groundwork for what would become the Aga Khan Development Network (AKDN) under the present Imam. As described in documents of the AKDN: "On the subcontinent of India and Pakistan, social development institutions were established, in the words of the late Aga Khan, 'for the relief of humanity.' They included institutions such as the Diamond Jubilee Trust and Platinum Jubilee Investments Limited, which in turn assisted the growth of various types of cooperative societies. Diamond Jubilee Schools for girls were established throughout the remote Northern Areas of what is now Pakistan. In addition, scholarship programmes, established at the time of the Golden Jubilee to give assistance to needy students, were progressively expanded. In East Africa, major social welfare and economic development institutions were established. Those involved in social welfare included the accelerated development of schools and community centres, and a modern, fully equipped hospital in Nairobi. Among the economic development institutions established in East Africa were companies such as the Diamond Jubilee Investment Trust (now the Diamond Trust of Kenya) and the Jubilee Insurance Company, which are quoted on the Nairobi Stock Exchange and have become major players in national development."[5] Aga Khan III also brought new organizational forms to the Ismailis, including a series of councils at local, national and regional levels that today represent the community for internal and external affairs. The English playwright and novelist W. Somerset Maugham wrote in his 'Forward' of the 1954 autobiography of Aga Khan III: "As head of a widely diffused sect, the Ismailis, he has throughout his life sedulously endeavoured to further the welfare, spiritual and material, of his countless followers."[6] Aga Khan III found it useful to have a single quote printed on an otherwise blank page at the beginning of the autobiography for which Maugham wrote the 'Forward': "Life is a great and noble calling, not a mean and grovelling thing to be shuffled through as best we can but a lofty and exalted destiny."[7] Expressed in terms easily comprehensible for the layman, this phrase is an expression of the Muslim concept of *din* and *dunya* (see page 29) which lies at the heart of the action of the Imamat.

Although vast regions were concerned by the social and economic development activities of Aga Khan III, most of these areas underwent significant political changes beginning with the independence of India and Pakistan from British rule in August 1947. So, too, countries with Ismaili populations such as Kenya (1963), Uganda (1962) and Tanganyika (which joined the islands of Zanzibar to form the United Republic of Tanzania in 1964) would be transformed during the Imamat of his successor. Indeed, the nomination of Aga Khan IV in 1957 brought unexpected changes in its own right, some of which were undoubtedly related to the rapid evolution of these parts of the world. Aga Khan III named as his successor neither his son, Prince Aly Khan (1911–60), nor the next in line, Prince Sadruddin Aga Khan (1933–2003). Instead, according to Aga Khan III's will, an excerpt of which was read to the press by his secretary after his death in 1957: "In view of the fundamentally altered conditions in the world in very recent years due to the great changes that have taken place, including the discoveries of atomic science, I am convinced that it is in the best interests of the Shia Muslim Ismaili community that I should be succeeded by a young man who has been brought up and developed during recent years and in the midst of the new age, and who brings a new outlook on life to his office."[8] This young man was Prince Karim Khan, born in 1936 in Geneva, the eldest son of Prince Aly Khan and his first wife, Princess Tajudowlah, formerly the Honourable Joan Guinness (1908–97). His nomination by his grandfather represented the first jump of a generation in the history of the Ismailis. Queen Elizabeth II granted Aga Khan IV the honorific title of 'His Highness' on 26 July 1957. One of his very early official tasks on 10 September 1958 was to inaugurate the fourteen-storey Aga Khan Platinum Jubilee Hospital in Nairobi, Kenya. One of the most modern facilities in Africa at the time, it was open to all races and religions, an idea initiated by his grandfather and enthusiastically embraced by the young Aga Khan. On the occasion of the inauguration, the Aga Khan declared: "The building must become a living monument to the ideal of racial partnership."[9]

Aga Khan III, aged seven, at his ceremony of accession as Imam of the Shia Ismaili Muslims, Bombay, India, 1 September 1885. He is surrounded by community elders.

A Prince for the World to Come

Prince Karim spent a good part of his childhood in Nairobi, Kenya, with his brother Prince Amyn, where both were tutored by a scholar from the Aligarh Muslim University (Aligarh, Uttar Pradesh, India). Prince Karim went on to attend the Institut Le Rosey (Rolle, Switzerland) and Harvard College in the United States, where he majored in Islamic Studies. As His Highness the Aga Khan reveals in the interview published in this book, he might well have preferred to study science at the Massachusetts Institute of Technology, but his grandfather felt that his future lay in the somewhat broader education offered by Harvard University, and in Islamic Studies. At the age of twenty, however, destiny intervened and the Aga Khan left Harvard for a far broader stage. What he discovered is related in the interview (in the following pages), but, clearly, the Imam was immediately faced with transformations on a global scale that affected his community both directly and indirectly. Some of these changes are described in a history of the Imamat: "In Africa, Asia and the Middle East, a major objective of the community's social welfare and economic programmes, until the mid 1950s, had been to create a broad base of businessmen, agriculturists and professionals. The educational facilities of the community tended to emphasize secondary-level education. With the coming of independence, each nation's economic aspirations took on new dimensions, focusing on industrialization and the modernization of agriculture. The community's educational priorities had to be reassessed in the context of new national goals, and new institutions had to be created to respond to the growing complexity of the development process."[10]

Although the Aga Khan found his community already very widely spread across the globe in 1957, events such as the 1972 expulsion of the Ismailis, indeed all Asians, from Uganda by President Idi Amin brought him to engage personally in a vast resettlement effort that led members of the community from Uganda, Tanzania, Kenya and Burma to make new homes in Asia, Europe and North America. The fact that Ismailis managed to build new lives in a relatively short span of time is certainly a testimony to their values and also to the strong and continued support of the Imam and the various community groups at all levels. Encouraged to engage their allegiance to their new countries in an active and responsible way, the displaced Ismailis found fewer difficulties than many other communities in similar circumstances. As had been the case in their countries of origin, Ismailis created community institutions in the West "characterized by an ethos of self-reliance, an emphasis on education and a pervasive spirit of philanthropy."[11] The origin of much of the construction work undertaken in more recent years by the Aga Khan may be found in the movement of this new Ismaili diaspora of the 1970s. Where the communities resettled and made their homes, he has made it his task to build Ismaili Centres and other buildings that emphasize the solidity and permanence of the Ismaili presence. These buildings serve the community but they also represent a symbolic investment in the respective countries involved, from Canada to Tajikistan.

As is public knowledge, the Aga Khan has engaged in numerous private activities, such as raising thoroughbred horses (part of a long family tradition), but he has also been actively involved in construction, and one of his early projects has bearing on his continued interest in architecture and development. Beginning in 1962, he created a resort community along fifty-six kilometres of rocky, pine-covered land on the north-east coast of the Island of Sardinia, in Italy. The Costa Smeralda, a 3000-hectare community, was built where nothing existed before apart from a few shepherd's houses. As the Aga Khan explains in the interview which follows this text, his approach there, beginning with an analysis of the land and then of the economic potential of the site, has served him well in subsequent projects, such as those led in more recent years by the Aga Khan Trust for Culture (AKTC). In a quest to maintain the cultural identity of the region, the houses and buildings erected on the site took the houses built by Sardinian shepherds – called *stazzu* – as their source of design inspiration. Plans were made not on the basis of immediate profitability but rather with the long-term development of the site in mind. As the Aga Khan points out, the Costa Smer-

Prince Karim Aga Khan, watching a procession from a reviewing stand during his ceremony of accession, 1 October 1957.

alda project differed from his actions as Imam in particular because the Sardinian resort was, after all, meant to generate profits, whereas that is not a goal of the community work he undertakes. Here in Sardinia, then, was architecture with a difference, where land planning, respect for the region and an eye to the long term took precedence over any superficial search for well-known architects, or, worse, the temptation to make a profit and then run, so typical of promoters the world over. Here, too, was a project on a scale that would prove useful when the question arose of how to best stimulate the economies of developing countries, of how to create value with architecture from nothing but a site.

A Network to Improve Lives

As tradition would have it, the Aga Khan's Silver Jubilee (July 1982–July 1983), marking his twenty-fifth anniversary as Imam, was the occasion for the launch of a number of projects, and to create new organizations. The first phase of the Aga Khan University and Teaching Hospital in Karachi, consisting of a 721-bed teaching hospital, a medical school for 500 students, a school of nursing and housing for students and staff, was completed in 1985, but begun several years earlier.

Schools for girls and medical centres in the remote Hunza Valley of northern Pakistan were launched; the Aga Khan Rural Support Programme in Pakistan and India was launched, as were extensions of existing urban hospitals and primary health-care centres in Tanzania and Kenya. New 'high-profile' Ismaili Centres in London (1981) and Burnaby, Vancouver (1984), were completed or underway. AKDN documents describe the Silver Jubilee projects as follows: "These initiatives form part of an international network of institutions involved in fields that range from education, health and rural development to architecture and the promotion of private-sector enterprise and together make up the Aga Khan Development Network. It is this commitment to man's dignity and relief of humanity that inspires the Ismaili Imamat's philanthropic institutions. Giving of one's competence, sharing one's time, material or intellectual wherewithal with those among whom one lives, for the relief of hardship, pain or ignorance is a deeply ingrained tradition which shapes the social conscience of the Ismaili Muslim community."[12]

The Aga Khan Development Network is the organization that groups the official, essentially non-religious activities of the Aga Khan. With a focus on health, education, culture, rural development, institution building and the promotion of economic development it cannot be said to place architecture as such in the forefront of its agenda. The Aga Khan, however, defines his interest in "the processes of change" (see interview on the following pages) as being directly related to the physical environment, and thus, in many senses, to the art of building. According to its own mission statement, the AKDN "is dedicated to improving living conditions and opportunities for the poor, without regard to their faith, origin or gender."[13]

The Aga Khan Development Network consists of nine distinct organizations, all of which are private and non-denominational.[14] Indeed, the clearest distinction that can be made between the specifically religious activities of the Aga Khan and his philanthropic organizations is precisely that the AKDN is intended to remain non-denominational. The AKDN is funded by the Aga Khan, but also by investments and grants from government, institutional and private-sector partners, as well as by donations from individuals. The Aga Khan also actively promotes philanthropic activity and the channelling of profits from commercial undertakings in support of social development and culture in developing and developed countries. The Aga Khan University is a private, autonomous international university, chartered by the government of Pakistan, while the Aga Khan Fund for Economic

Development is incorporated as a commercial entity under Swiss law. The University of Central Asia was established by an international treaty registered by the United Nations. The other agencies are incorporated in Switzerland as non-profit institutions. The work of the AKDN is concentrated in South and Central Asia and East Africa, in areas inhabited largely by very poor populations, but the organizations are also present throughout much of the Islamic world and in specific cases in Europe, North America or elsewhere.

The scope and purpose of this book clearly does not cover all of the activities of the AKDN, despite the broad definition of architecture given by His Highness the Aga Khan. And yet, where architecture does not seem to be the primary concern, in education for example, the Aga Khan Education Services, the Aga Khan Foundation, the Aga Khan University, the Aga Khan Academies and the University of Central Asia all have a significant interest in the subject. In some instances, single architects have been given enormous responsibility, as is the case of Tom Payette of Boston for the Aga Khan University, or Arata Isozaki from Tokyo for the new University of Central Asia. It seems apparent that the essential link between these activities, and many others, is the Aga Khan himself and his stated interest in the improvement of the physical environment.

One significant example of the activities of the Aga Khan Development Network is the Aga Khan Planning and Building Service (AKPBS) established in 1980 with a mandate to plan and implement infrastructure and technology-related development initiatives to improve the built environment and to enhance living conditions for the most vulnerable and disadvantaged populations. It provides material, technical assistance and applied research, as well as planning and construction management services for communities in both rural and urban areas. The objectives of the Aga Khan Planning and Building Service have been inspired by the Aga Khan's belief that "a proper home can provide the bridge across that terrible gulf between poverty and a better future." The agency has developed more than sixty low-cost, seismic-resistant, energy and resource efficient housing construction methods and standards.

Another agency, more than the others, however, has had a direct and continued involvement in the search for excellence in architecture and in the restoration of monuments in the Islamic world. That agency is the Aga Khan Trust for Culture (AKTC). Created from 1988 onwards, "the Trust focuses on the physical, social, cultural and economic revitalization of communities in the Muslim world. It includes the Aga Khan Award for Architecture, the Historic Cities Programme, the Music Initiative in Central Asia, the online resource ArchNet, and the Aga Khan Program for Islamic Architecture at Harvard University and the Massachusetts Institute of Technology."[15] Currently under the direction of Luis Monreal, the AKTC has assumed a central role insofar as the built environment figures in the overall initiatives of the Aga Khan. Monreal's globe-straddling experience and culture have allowed the Aga Khan Trust for Culture to advance even more rapidly than it had in the past, implementing large projects such as Azhar Park in Cairo and

Above, a view of the facade of the Ismaili Centre and Jamatkhana in London, United Kingdom.

Left, a detail of the Ismaili Centre and Jamatkhana in Burnaby, British Columbia, Canada.

taking on new projects, from the Aga Khan Museum in Toronto to the study of the music of the Silk Road, with equal expertise and mastery. The story of the development of the programmes of the AKTC, and in particular of the Aga Khan Award for Architecture, illustrates the commitment and far-reaching thought behind the institutions. As might be expected, however, the AKTC does not stand alone in the complex and wide-ranging activities of the Aga Khan. His continued involvement in construction has both nourished the Award and drawn from its lessons. It is clear that the Aga Khan's actual construction activity, apart from private projects, has frequently involved his role as Imam. A pertinent example of architecture related to the concomitant roles of the AKDN and the Imamat is the Delegation of the Ismaili Imamat building presently under construction in Ottawa, Canada. Designed by the noted Japanese architect Fumihiko Maki, the building will be used by both the AKDN and the Imamat. As the Aga Khan declared in 2005: "The Delegation will serve a representational role for the Imamat and its non-denominational, philanthropic and development agencies which constitute the Aga Khan Development Network – the AKDN. An open, secular facility, the Delegation will be a sanctuary for peaceful, quiet diplomacy, informed by the Imamat's outlook of global convergence and the development of civil society. It will be an enabling venue for fruitful public engagements, information services and educational programmes, all backed up by high-quality research, to sustain a vibrant intellectual centre, and a key policy-informing institution."[16] Other activities, such as the construction of Ismaili Centres from Vancouver to Dushanbe, concern the Imamat directly, rather than the AKDN, because these are religious buildings. And yet, the underlying and unifying force behind the AKDN and the Imamat is of course the Aga Khan himself.

Although the Aga Khan can and must act through his institutions, and, indeed, ultimately his power springs from the faith of the Ismaili community itself, he has always sought out particularly qualified individuals from varied horizons, who have worked for him, given their opinions and in some cases helped to shape the course of events. In the final analysis, the real story of the involvement of the Aga Khan in architecture is one of people. First and foremost, these are the people that he has sought from the first to assist – the poor of his community and beyond, those of the Muslim world – but also the people he has worked with in whatever capacity. The contents of this book are derived in large part from discussions with some of those who have mattered in the evolution of institutions, such as the Aga Khan Award for Architecture and the Aga Khan Program for Islamic Architecture (AKPIA), or who have worked in one capacity or another for His Highness. As should become apparent in these interviews, one project of the Aga Khan very often led to another; as the Costa Smeralda opened vistas, so, too, did the projects undertaken thereafter by the Aga Khan, in particular the Aga Khan University in Karachi. Processes of thought and the construction not only of buildings, but also of institutions and educational tools such as the AKPIA at Harvard and MIT, could also be considered an integral part of the unique approach of the Aga Khan to architecture. The sum of these many parts might best be described as a definition of the Aga Khan's own way of describing architecture – "the processes of change." The sum of a number of interviews is not sufficient to explain every form of involvement of this one man with architecture nor, even more clearly, with the physical environment. A more modest goal might be to better understand a process of thought and its results.

From the Earth to the Sky

It is apparent from descriptions of his activities that the Aga Khan had a considerable interest in the physical environment from the commencement of his Imamat. This interest was translated into a hands-on approach to construction in school or hospital projects, but also with the Costa Smeralda development. Gerald Wilkinson, who served for some years as head of the Information Department of the Secretariat of the Aga Khan, confirms this view. "He was acutely interested in architecture from the early days. In the 1960s, when he was travelling in Pakistan, he made speeches that had to do with avoiding excessive influence from Western architecture, and this was around the time of the development of Islamabad as the new capital.[17] He inherited a building in Nairobi that was not finished when his grandfather died called the Platinum Jubilee Hospital. Although it won a RIBA award, it has terrible failings.[18] I suspect that he felt that in the future he was going to be involved in building designs."[19] Wilkinson affirms that the Costa Smeralda project played a role in forming the architectural acumen of the Aga Khan: "In Sardinia, in the early 1960s, he was only twenty-four or twenty-five, but one of the first things he did was to set up an architectural committee which was the governing body for design. Frankly, Sardinia had no architectural heritage to speak of. He developed a style that some criticized, but he was able to establish a sense of unity." Wilkinson, who worked on the Costa Smeralda project from 1979 to 1982, recalls: "At the beginning of my work there, he would come down and spend about four or five days in Sardinia, and he would devote himself a hundred per cent to Sardinia. Part of these sessions, in which I participated, was devoted to architecture. On one occasion, there was a Cuban architect, Elena Suarez, who had produced plans for a new residential development. He looked at these rather technical plans and immediately said that it was unsatisfactory for people to come out of their apartments onto a corridor balcony and have no view." Gerald Wilkinson concludes: "All of these things, the fact that he inherited a building in progress, that he was involved in a lot of community building on a smaller scale, and then the fact that he jumped into Sardinia, and felt it was his responsibility to be the judge of what was good in architectural terms…" had an impact on his way of dealing with the built environment.[20]

One of the trusted partners in developments undertaken by the Aga Khan beginning in the 1960s was the American firm Sasaki Associates. Based in Watertown, Massachusetts, the firm was founded in 1953 by Hideo Sasaki, who had studied at the University of California at Berkeley, the University of Illinois, and at Harvard. From 1958 to 1968, Sasaki served as Chairman of Harvard's Landscape Architecture Department. His firm was involved from the first in the study of the Costa Smeralda site. As Don Olson, a former Principal of Sasaki, explains: "We began work on Costa Smeralda with our firm in 1968. There were four architects, each working on a different hotel, or site, on the peninsula. There was no master plan so we were brought in to pick up with what had been established thus far and to try to develop an overall plan, so that the infrastructure itself could take on a logical growth – roads, water, sewage and so on."[21] Sasaki was introduced to the Aga Khan through Morgan Wheelock, who worked with the firm from 1964 to 1978 and who had attended Harvard College at the same time as Prince Amyn Aga Khan, the younger brother of Prince Karim.[22] In a more subjective tone, Don Olson describes his personal view of the ways in which the Aga Khan worked on projects in which he was involved: "He is moulding and guiding the process where the architecture is concerned. I have sat with him during meetings where he asked architects about things they had changed in their plans – he sees all the details. He likes certain things, but does not always know why he likes them. I believe that in these circumstances he responds to

A walkway in Azhar Park, Cairo, Egypt, looking from the Hilltop Restaurant toward the Citadel in the distance.

the initiatives of others. He is not going to get out a pencil and start drawing. If they change it, he wants to know why. He is more ready to accept changes if they are for regulatory or structural reasons, but, if it is purely a question of design, he may take a stronger stance. The architects he likes are generally the ones who are open to explain what they are doing."[23]

While Sasaki was working on the Costa Smeralda project, they also got involved in developing the master plan for a property purchased by the Aga Khan in Gouvieux, France. Aiglemont was to become a centre for the Secretariat of the Aga Khan as well as his personal residence. At this point, another figure from Sasaki came on board. Garr Campbell, a landscape architect, met the Aga Khan for the first time in early 1971. He had just obtained his Master's degree in Landscape Architecture at the Harvard Graduate School of Design. One of his first assignments was to work on a Thoroughbred Training Centre at Aiglemont, followed by the Aiglemont master plan. He soon left Sasaki's and "joined His Highness's small staff as a landscape architect. Initially, my assignment at Aiglemont was the implementation of the master plan, site design and planting." The landscape work undertaken by Garr Campbell was carried out in harmony with a series of buildings designed by Pierre Barbe, who was the winner of a 1973 competition for the architecture of the complex. Barbe carried out this work between that year and 1980.[24] Campbell went on to do work on another major project, the Aga Khan Hospital and University in Karachi. He was also in charge of design management at the Burnaby Ismaili Centre, a member of the Board of Directors for the construction of the London Ismaili Centre, and worked on the original concept plan for Azhar Park in Cairo. Just as he had in Sardinia, the Aga Khan paid careful attention in all of these cases to the sites involved – to the land itself – and in this he differentiated himself from many other clients.

Garr Campbell also played a role in another nascent project that was to be a centrepiece of the Aga Khan's next step in the architectural world. He explains: "In 1976 Michael Curtis, who was the principal aid of the Aga Khan, asked me what I thought of His Highness starting an Architectural Award. The Award was clearly His Highness's idea. Early on, before the Award became a public entity, I went to Boston to visit Professor James Ackerman at Harvard, whom I had known when I was a graduate student. Professor Ackerman is a very distinguished Italian Renaissance art historian. He strongly recommended Professor Oleg Grabar as the right person to advise His Highness regarding the Islamic Architecture Award, as it was called at the time. Oleg Grabar recommended that I also talk to Professor William Porter at MIT and Professor Renata Holod of the University of Pennsylvania. I recall that Professor Porter was also recommended by Tom Payette. These were some of the first steps in the creation of the Award. That was my role. I was graciously invited to attend the Steering Committee Meetings and for the First Award Cycle my name was included as a member of the Steering Committee."[25] The ties of the Aga Khan to Harvard, where he attended college, and the Massachusetts Institute of Technology, were he had initially been admitted to undergraduate studies, are clear, but, through figures such as Garr Campbell and other key participants in the development of the Award, the connection to the two Cambridge institutions became one of the underpinnings not only of the Award, but of future programmes such as the Aga Khan Program for Islamic Architecture. As to the motivations behind the clear interest of the Aga Khan in landscape design, Garr Campbell writes: "I suspect that the Aga Khan's interest in landscape and building has been with him from an early age. His interest was cultivated most likely from his family, European residence and heritage, as well as travelling widely. I doubt that I had much to do with those interests. He very subtly guided me in the direction he wished to go. I did not impose anything that was not his objective. He had a very clear idea of what he wanted … His interest in high-quality, subtle landscape is very sophisticated. There seems to be a search for appropriate cultural and natural solutions in the various development projects His Highness has undertaken. His interest in landscape as a context for buildings, I assume, is to create a place of tranquillity and beauty, islands of calm in an otherwise very chaotic and hostile world."[26]

Two views of the Aga Khan University in Karachi, Pakistan, designed by Payette Associates of Boston.

A Modern Vision of Architecture for the Islamic World

The events leading up to the creation of the Aga Khan Award for Architecture and, later, the Aga Khan Program for Islamic Architecture at Harvard and MIT most definitely included the design and construction of the Aga Khan University and Teaching Hospital in Karachi. Consisting of a 721-bed teaching hospital, a medical school for 500 students, a school of nursing, housing for staff and students, all built on an original twenty-six-hectare site donated by the government of Pakistan, the facility was designed in 1972–73, and completed in 1985. The Aga Khan University (AKU) has undergone substantial expansions since that date, and an even larger project, the Faculty of Arts and Sciences, is presently in the planning process. It is surely significant that the AKU complex, right up to its present development, is essentially the work of a single architectural firm, that of Tom Payette in Boston. Payette's recollection of the beginnings of the project is of interest. "It was in 1970 or 1971. They had a programme for the medical school, hospital and nursing school project in Karachi. Arthur D. Little did the first assessment of what you would do for a medical school and hospital complex. The Economics Intelligence Unit that is part of *The Economist* magazine was engaged to provide management for the project and in turn they hired Dr David Gray, who was Head Hospital Programmer for the Ministry of Health in the United Kingdom. After visiting the Platinum Jubilee Hospital in Nairobi, Dr Gray was responsible for the development of the programme for the hospital and medical school. Devon Twelves, an architect from the English Ministry of Health, also had an early role in its planning. A committee with representation from the Ministry of Health and the *Economist* group was formed and they were supposed to select architects to interview mainly from Germany, France, the United Kingdom and the United States. There was one American on the committee, Morgan Wheelock. Morgan was a partner in Sasaki. I came to work for a firm in Boston in 1960 that specialized in hospitals. The gentlemen from Markus and Nocka hired me.[27] In 1965, I landed a substantial project, the Leonard Morse Hospital in Natick, Massachusetts. One morning at breakfast in Morgan Wheelock's home, he suggested I should be interviewed for the Karachi project. A year later, they had interviewed firms in Europe, and then they came to Boston to interview the Architects Collaborative. They had 250 people, and we had about forty. I took the committee to Leonard Morse Hospital, and ten days later I got a call and they put two conditions on my being considered: one was that I should work with the engineers Parsons Brown and that we should create a partnership with them for that purpose. I knew who the client was but I did not know much about him. I only knew that he was at Harvard when he became the Aga Khan in 1957, and that he went away for a year. Morgan had worked for him. They also asked me to work with a man called Mozhan Khadem. I was to engage him as a design consultant for the Islamic world. He was an Iranian impregnated with Islamic culture."[28] It is apparent in this description both that the Aga Khan was certain to surround himself with highly competent and specialized consultants when embarking on the design of a new hospital and teaching facility, and that his search for a modern vision of architecture and Islam was central to his thinking. Then, too, he was not afraid to call on an architect who admittedly had no experience of the Muslim world. Tom Payette was, rather, a man who could listen.

Payette continues: "His Highness came to visit us in Boston before we had the contract. Michael Curtis came with him. I did a presentation and we got in his limousine and I took him to Leonard Morse Hospital. We went through the hospital and he asked questions. His Highness then stood in front of the hospital and said: 'Mr Payette this is a terrific hospital, but it is not anything that

I want.' He did not say any more than that. Two days later, I got a letter telling me I could do the job. He felt that I would listen, and that I would look, and that I would undertake to try to find a direction that would relate in a modern way to Islam. We opened an office in London and His Highness would meet us there every month."[29] At the instigation of the Aga Khan and in the company of Mozhan Khadem, Payette and others now involved in the project took a one-month tour of the Islamic world. They started in Spain, went to North Africa, Beirut, Isfahan and finally to Karachi. Payette's straightforward manner, undoubtedly a quality that is appreciated by the Aga Khan, comes through clearly in his brief description of what he learned in Karachi, what he accomplished there, and what he hopes to continue to do with the new Faculty of Arts and Sciences for the Aga Khan University: "I am approaching thirty-five years of continuous work on the original campus and now we are starting the Faculty of Arts and Sciences.

The Aga Khan University opened up a whole new world for a little guy who came from Michigan. All of those buildings, with the exception of the lecture halls and the housing, are on a 6.7-metre grid. All with a system of concrete structure that allows many variations. They are modern buildings in an interesting way. They use a lot of contemporary thought about space, and the flexibility of systems. The outside skin is stucco. The windows are set back to encourage natural ventilation. The skin is white cement that is pigmented. It covers up imperfections, but, above all, when the sun hits it, it takes the glare away. We used all kinds of techniques related to human comfort. The wainscoting is in Pakistani marble for example. It creates a rich pattern. His Highness says that the original AKU campus still looks new after more than twenty years. The architecture is modern or modernist, but at the same time deeply rooted in the culture. This is not theatre decor. It has to do with how people inhabit the climate. The idea of the continuity of space within a perimeter is not modern but ancient."[30] The qualities of Payette's architecture, and, indeed, his way of describing the project, highlight characteristics that the Aga Khan had already shown in other circumstances – his concern for the well-being of patients, or students in this case; and his desire for modernity impregnated with Islamic values without being a pastiche or "theatre decor", as Payette puts it. In Payette's story there also emerges a better understanding of how given individuals have helped to form the links between one project and the next. Thus, Morgan Wheelock of Sasaki Associates played a role in bringing Tom Payette to the attention of the Aga Khan. When he was asked his opinion on the potential for an architecture award in 1976, Tom Payette suggested that university involvement should be a priority and proposed to approach William Porter,[31] who at the time was Dean of the School of Architecture at MIT.

Though it is obvious that certain individuals have played a significant role in the development of the programmes of the Aga Khan, the origins of one of his central initiatives in the area of architecture clearly lie with his own questions about the physical environment of Islam. On the occasion of the First Seminar of the Aga Khan Award for Architecture held at Aiglemont in April 1978, the Aga Khan gave a clear indication of his motivations in establishing the Award: "The community that I lead is small but widespread. It is in daily contact with a multitude of Muslim societies, nationalities and languages, and with an increasingly diverse number of non-Muslim peoples and countries. It therefore experiences as wide a number of exchanges of physical, cultural and linguistic exposures as any other Muslim community. It is as a result of my community's experience that I have been haunted by one single question: what is the future physical environment that Muslims should seek for themselves and future generations in their homelands, their institutions, their workplaces, their houses, their gardens, and in their surroundings? I am a Muslim who has been in the position to build schools, housing complexes and hospitals, for Ismailis and non-Ismailis alike. While I am confident that I can determine the types of education I wish to provide in the schools, the living standards in the housing complexes or the level of medical care in the hospitals, I find that I am unable to give clear directives to any architect for the creation of an equally soundly conceived and appropriate design solution. While each new institution has an individual purpose, as it should, there are few design objectives and even fewer solutions which could become an inspiration for others."[32] So, too, the experience he was gaining with the Aga Khan University in Karachi played a role in inspiring the creation of the Award that he rendered explicit in the same speech: "I have had recent practical experience with this problem in the development of a 700-bed teaching hospital in Karachi. One of my requirements was that the resulting design should reflect the spirit of Islam. By this I do not mean a soulless mimicry of past traditions of architecture, but a generation of new design, using the aesthetic and practical bases of these traditions."[33]

A 1979 meeting of the Steering Committee for the First Cycle of the Aga Khan Award for Architecture. Seated at the middle of the image, His Highness the Aga Khan. To his right, Renata Holod; to his left, Oleg Grabar and William Porter.

A Source of Inspiration for Others

The Aga Khan Award for Architecture was officially established in 1977. It is intended to "recognize examples of architectural excellence that encompass contemporary design, social housing, community improvement and development, restoration, reuse, and area conservation, as well as landscaping and environmental issues." Organized on the basis of three-year cycles, the Award is governed by a Steering Committee chaired by the Aga Khan. The Award "seeks to identify and encourage building concepts that successfully address the needs and aspirations of societies in which Muslims have a significant presence."[34] The Award has completed nine cycles of activity since 1977, and documentation has been compiled on over 7500 building projects located throughout the world. In the nature of projects selected, in the emphasis placed on social issues and even in the credit given to clients for bringing buildings to life, the Aga Khan Award has little to do with other prizes in the field. It is in a class by itself, one imagined by the Aga Khan with the support and thought of a well-rounded group of pioneers assembled around him. One of these figures was Oleg Grabar.[35] As he recalls the early days of the Award: "I was a Professor at Harvard, and I received a phone call from Bill Porter, who was Dean at MIT, and we had lunch with Garr Campbell. I was told that the Aga Khan was planning an award for architecture and I was asked if I would join the project. I went to Paris with Bill Porter and Garr Campbell – perhaps Hugh Casson[36] was there and Michael Curtis. We invented the notion of the Steering Committee. I believe it was in 1976. Nader Ardalan[37] and Hassan Fathy[38] were asked to join shortly afterwards. Hugh Casson suggested we look for a 'convenor.' I suggested Renata Holod who had been a student of mine. We agreed that she should be seconded by a Muslim man, and Hasan Uddin Khan was selected. They were very good people who worked well together. Charles Correa also joined the committee quite early. The Aga Khan was part of it, and he was extremely generous. The group was remarkable, and we felt we were inventing something together. Renata and Hasan made trips all over the world. They brought back things that were fresh and new. There was a first seminar near Paris in 1978. I remember driving back to the city from Chantilly, and I was sitting next to an Egyptian minister who said that he had been going to international meetings for years and that for the first time he was proud to be a Muslim."[39] Grabar is too cosmopolitan and learned to be in any way condescending. He, too, was proud to be a part of this innovative effort.

Another participant in the early meetings organized by the Aga Khan, William Porter from MIT, also shared his recollections of the creation of the Award: "The Aga Khan was on a search – he had not decided what was appropriate. I never felt that he had made up his mind in advance about the process or how it was all going to come out. He was interested in hearing what the individuals around that table thought. He was there to listen and to provoke. He was impatient with what was happening – the cheap, opportunistic knock-offs of Western designs with no respect for tradition being built in the Gulf, for example. His position was what I would call angst about having architecture that could speak to and about the Muslim world. This was not a game about trying to set up a nice Award; it was much more about what the cultural role of architecture could be, and how it could best be realized. The first Steering Committee meetings were the venue in which these conversations took place. In the less formal meetings, it might be fair to say that His Highness, Oleg Grabar and I had more to say than the other members. Renata Holod was one of Oleg's students, so she was quite influential in the early phase."[40]

The Aga Khan Award for Architecture and More

When she was contacted by Michael Curtis at the suggestion of Oleg Grabar and William Porter in 1977, Renata Holod was an Assistant Professor in the History of Art Department at the University of Pennsylvania.[41] Indeed, it appeared that Professor Holod was ideally suited to becoming involved in the nascent Award. She says: "In 1977 I had already taught four years of architectural history for architects. The Aga Khan said there was a problem in getting architects to think about where they are building. 'How,' he asked, 'do you connect the old traditions of architecture with the new?' This was precisely how I was teaching the history of architecture to my students. Most architects are not interested in whether a building was built in 1076 or in 1079. You have to talk to them about the nature of the building. What is the nature of the design and in what context does it sit? I told the Aga Khan I understood what he meant."[42] As for the definition of the Award at the time she was called on, Renata Holod recalls: "It was still very vague. Another person who had been working with His Highness at the time, Ian Robertson, had been involved in the Aga Khan University project in Karachi. They were just beginning this idea of building something. The hospital was really at the origin of this idea of how to get architects working in these countries to think about the fact that they are building there, and not in New York or Paris. I remember these issues were constantly being talked about at the time – in terms of the nature of culture-friendly design, of 'rootedness' – which today seem to be normal issues, but at the time, they were not." While the intellectual basis for creating the Award was the Aga Khan's fundamental interrogation about modern ways to build in the Muslim world, the mechanisms of the Award remained to be created. According to Dr Holod: "I was supposed to find myself an assistant, and I found Hasan Uddin Khan. Because I was familiar with Morocco and Syria and Iran and Turkey, we needed someone who was familiar with the subcontinent. Because I was an archaeologist and an architectural historian, it was useful that he should be an architect. The date for the first Award was set for 1980 – so we had two years to prepare. I rented two rooms in the University City Science Centre in Philadelphia. We went off on a series of trips in March 1978. Every two weeks we met with the Executive Committee – we would propose something and they would look at it. Everything – from the wording for the Award to the way in which it was supposed to run – came into being this way. We designed everything you see now – the technical reviewers, the length of the cycle. All the apparatus was proposed, discussed and fixed. We ran a series of seminars – that was actually the most important and exciting part about the whole process. We had the first seminar in Aiglemont, the second in Istanbul, the third in Jakarta, the fourth in Fez and the fifth in Amman.

The Egyptian architect Hassan Fathy at his drafting table in 1980. Fathy was a member of the first Steering Committee.

Hasan Uddin Khan and I travelled from Morocco to Indonesia. For each trip the idea was to meet with the Chamber of Architects and the Ministries of Urbanism or Culture, and this is how we developed the network. I remember arriving in Indonesia with one telephone number. My former students were spread all over the world and that is how we began the network. After each of these trips we prepared country reports. The idea of regional nominators was in it from the first – as was the principle that it would be for built projects and not for designed or planned projects."[43]

Just as the Costa Smeralda project or the Aga Khan University in Karachi had their impact on future developments in the organizations of the Aga Khan, so, in an even more fruitful way, did the Award. Renata Holod describes the early days in the creation of the Award in fervent terms, and returns to the seminal influence of the AKU in Karachi: "The start-up phase was exciting because everybody was being shaken up. It was all at the instigation of the Aga Khan, and he was playing a key role in the development of the language of the categories, of the descriptions of the early seminars. He made impromptu speeches, much more so at the beginning than subsequently, when all of these other ideas that have developed as separate programmes were initially part of the Award. The educational component, the seminars; then came the idea: if you think this is such an important thing, why don't you put your own money into it? We went to Cairo – Azhar Park was announced in 1984, I think. The Award was like a huge centrifuge. Let's do public education, let's do a film. ArchNet began because all of this material had to be made available to a larger audience. *Mimar*[44] too was a spin-off. The Historic Cities Support Programme, the Harvard-MIT education programme (AKPIA) – they were all being talked about right from the beginning. The Aga Khan Program for Islamic Architecture was installed right after the Award. His Highness was right there. How do you set up this sort of thing? What is development? What is the large scale or the small scale? How do you make a programme? The real beginning goes back to the Aga Khan University in Karachi, before I arrived. That is how the whole thing started. How do you build something that is useful and has an impact, and how do you transfer that experience to a larger audience? If you cannot do it, maybe there are structural ways in which you can influence the way you form the next generation that could do other things."

Hasan Uddin Khan, who was first the assistant to Renata Holod as 'Convenor' of the Aga Khan Award for Architecture, and then her successor, raises a different point of view about the Award and about other initiatives of the Aga Khan. What was the Aga Khan seeking when he created the Award? "He said it was to encourage Muslims to look anew at their own situation and create a contemporary architecture for their societies. I believe the hospital in Karachi was extremely important to him. Payette was sent on a journey around the Islamic world because His Highness was interested in finding an appropriate architecture. In Muslim countries at the time, they were either doing historicist things with domes and arches or very modern buildings, and the Aga Khan felt that there needed to be some kind of synthesis. He said he wanted to develop something that you could intellectually defend as belonging to the country and the culture and that was contemporary at the same time."[45] These goals are clearly inspired by the very nature of the Imamat and the personality of the Aga Khan. Might it not have been, however, that the long history that led the present Aga Khan to his programmes would have led him to privilege tradition more than contemporary architecture? Hasan Uddin Khan replies: "He said you have to understand your tradition. I never got the impression that he wanted to create new buildings that were going to be traditional in any sense. We had a discussion in the early days when he said that we must look at historic environments. One of the awards was eventually for restoration and adaptive reuse. Understanding the past and understanding urban environments becomes very important in the attempt to build a new architecture. Public housing was also very important to him, but it was hard to find good projects – the same is true for industrial buildings."[46] Hasan Uddin Khan feels that one of the most significant aspects of the Aga Khan Award for Architecture was the early decision to include for consideration only buildings that had been completed for at least two years. This, he says, was very much against the architectural discourse of the time. "I think," he concludes, "that that is one of the most powerful things the Award has done – to say that a building is about the architect, but that it is also about the client and the use of the building."[47]

In the early 1980s, Hasan Uddin Khan was also directly involved in another of the architectural initiatives of the Aga Khan, the magazine *Mimar: Architecture in Development*, which remains one of the most highly respected and influential journals in its field, despite having halted publication some years ago. He describes the rapport between the creation of the Award and that of the magazine: "Renata Holod left the Award just before the first ceremony, so I took over at that time. I was in Lahore for the first awards. I read the citations and I passed His Highness the statue. It was quite simple. It became much more sophisticated afterwards. I felt that the Islamic world did not have any good architecture publication – there were local ones, but nothing broader. I went to His Highness and said we really need a publication. He agreed, but immediately said that he wanted it separate from the Award. I proposed a magazine that would look at the developing world in general and would have an emphasis on Islamic societies. The things we needed to look at might include what was happening in South America or India, where Islam was not involved. I was introduced to Brian Taylor. He had worked for the magazine *AD*, but not for His Highness. Brian was quite excited. We set it up together. He introduced me to Emilio Ambasz.[48] I wanted to produce a mock-up. I had no idea of economics or distribution, but I felt that developing countries should not have a cheap newspaper. I wanted to out-gloss anything that was being published. I thought that what was important was the image – that people who read other architecture journals would recognize *Mimar* as a magazine of the same standard and quality as the best. It had to be visually exciting because architects like visually exciting things. We came up with the idea of the cut-out based on a Mughal miniature – Emilio designed the first two covers himself."[49]

As it happens, there was some disenchantment with *Mimar* and indeed its publication was suspended, in part because it was not reaching a sufficiently large audience. In 1998 the Aga Khan told Oleg Grabar that he was disappointed that what he described as the "new cultural consciousness, the new sense of the importance of tradition and ethical issues surrounding its conservation and preservation, had so far been limited to a small and elite group of intellectuals and professionals in the Muslim societies most directly affected by the changes in question, as well as by the attitudes toward them." In his opinion *Mimar* was "too elite a voice and a publication for the expression of the concerns of history, tradition and identity raised by the Award. It quite simply did not reach enough people because it was too expensive."[50] This is one of the reasons for the creation of the ArchNet website based at MIT in 1998 (see page 146). After a hiatus of several years during which the failure of *Mimar* was studied, it became apparent that the Internet offered the kind of broad accessibility that was sought by the Aga Khan.

Architecture for Men, Women and Children

The history of the organization of the Aga Khan Award for Architecture is significant insofar as it reveals the goals to be attained and the methods employed. It also demonstrates the extent to which the Aga Khan pursued his own interrogations with the able assistance of those mentioned here and

MIMAR 1 · 1981

*Mimar 1: Architecture
in Development*,
July–September 1981,
cover designed by
Emilio Ambasz.

many others. But mechanism and organization are really not the issue. The goal, one might say the dream, that the Aga Khan has pursued consistently in his rapport with architecture can be clearly linked to his role as Imam, but, more, to his profound spiritual awareness, and thus to his sense of indispensable pluralism. What makes the Aga Khan Award for Architecture different from any other prize of its type was expressed by its founder at the Presentation Ceremony for the first Award in 1980. Referring to some of the projects selected, he stated: "This recognition of a human scale, of local decisions, of local needs and concerns is, I believe, a profoundly Muslim requirement. It is the expression of that social concern for thousands of separate communities within the whole *umma* which is so uniquely a central part of the Muslim message. We have recognized an architecture for men, women and children, not yet an architecture for history books and tourists. Through architecture, we are recognizing the quality of life within the Muslim world *today*. And, by recognizing a housing project developed by a whole community or a medical centre, we are preserving for all times the memory of this quality of life."[51] It is precisely the search for an architecture that is not yet "for history books and tourists" that makes the Aga Khan Award significant. Nor does the Aga Khan restrict the nature of this search and its potential lessons to the Muslim world: "And finally, we may turn from the Muslim world to the whole world. Many of the issues which led to the creation of the Awards are not unique to the Muslim world. They are issues found in all new lands, as on our shrinking planet all new countries, or all developing countries, grope for a visible self-identification of their own and for the satisfaction of new, worldwide expectations about the quality of their lives. But why think only of new or developing countries? Social problems plague lands with the highest per capita income, and self-identification is a concern of countries with the longest history of independence and expansion. It may be just that, as the Award highlights the search of the Muslim world for an architecture centred on man and proclaiming the potential of life, an example is given to the whole world of how this can be done. In part it is simply that the Muslim message is a universal one and not restricted to a few areas or a few ethnic groups. But in a deeper sense, what we are trying to achieve, this environment we are looking for, is not only ours. It is also something we want to share with the whole world, not as an exercise in pride or vanity, but because of our belief that the means at our disposal may allow us to sharpen the issues, to discover solutions for all mankind to use and understand."[52]

Education at the Highest Level

As a number of participants in the development of the Aga Khan's programmes in architecture have confirmed, the idea of creating chairs in Islamic art and architecture at Harvard University and the Massachusetts Institute of Technology grew almost directly out of the Aga Khan Award for Architecture. This was all the more the case because William Porter from MIT and Oleg Grabar from Harvard were instrumental figures in giving form to both ideas. In Porter's words: "The path that led from talking about architecture and what the institutions were that one has to engage in all inexorably led to the question of education. The model of how architecture of importance might be recognized was applied to how education of importance might be developed. You do not shy away from the Western model but you do not fall victim to its formulae. When I first went to the school in

Ahmedabad where Balkrishna Doshi had been teaching[53] there were pictures of Western buildings on the walls. His students were working on the notion of architecture as an international skill that involved the use of *inappropriate* construction materials. By inappropriate I mean materials that might have to be foreign bought, manipulated by foreign engineers, or marketed by people who can rip off profits. This is the idea of exploitation by importation. Under Doshi's influence this attitude was giving way to an attempt to understand the architecture of the local area. When you create a

model of how to recognize an architecture that is appropriate to a region, one that is not too heavily dependent on the West, that is also a model that the Aga Khan was comfortable with. His contribution to Harvard and MIT was made in the hope that those recognized institutions might be able to teach the teachers who, later on in their areas, would contribute to the advancement of appropriate architectural models."[54] Oleg Grabar confirms that he and William Porter were the instruments of a will clearly expressed by the Aga Khan. "He is the one who called Bill Porter and me to have breakfast with him in Istanbul one day. He said he realized that he had to do something for higher education and he asked us for a proposal for Harvard and MIT. He had studied at Harvard and had applied to MIT and was accepted there too. He genuinely liked Bill Porter and me. The universities helped us but they did not believe it would work. At the St Botolphe Club, in Boston, we had a meeting with His Highness and a lunch with Derek Bok[55] and Jerome Wiesner[56] and I think Michael Curtis. The Aga Khan immediately told them that the investment required to create a dual programme in their universities

In the enormous and often dusty urban sprawl of Cairo, Egypt, the green spaces of Azhar Park provide welcome relief for city dwellers.

would pose no problem."[57] The Aga Khan confirms the relationship of the Award to the Aga Khan Program for Islamic Architecture (AKPIA) in a 2001 interview: "As the Award continued, we ended up by having to accept the fact that we needed to communicate; we needed to have an impact on values – ethical and aesthetic value judgments – and we needed to impact cultural value judgments; therefore, we had to impact opinion leaders. The second thing we had to do was to accept reality. That reality was that the industrialized world was dominating the processes of change in the Third World, in particular in the Islamic world. And that domination resulted in an educational process, or educational processes, in the Islamic world, and in the Third World generally, which were First-World driven. Therefore, we had to accept that an educational role was necessary. We committed that the primary educational role was not going to be that of the Award, because the Award did not want to become a school, but the need for education was real. That became the basis for the Aga Khan Program for Islamic Architecture at Harvard University and the Massachusetts Institute of Technology."[58]

The Processes Required to Achieve Change

Another initiative that grew out of the Award was the Historic Cities Support Programme (recently renamed the Historic Cities Programme). Although some restoration work (Zafra House, Granada, Spain, 1991) was carried out earlier under the auspices of the Aga Khan Award for Architecture, it appeared around the same time that an independent organization should be created for this kind of hands-on work on historic monuments, as opposed to the observer status of the Award itself. Both the HCSP (now the HCP) and the Award were grouped together after 1992 in the Aga Khan Trust for Culture (AKTC). One of the early managers of the AKTC was John de Monchaux.[59] He recalls: "My wife, who is a behavioural scientist and urban planner, and I carried out programme design study for what was to become the Aga Khan Trust for Culture, and I did a programme design study for His Highness looking at what was to become the HCSP. We interviewed His Highness and other members of the Aga Khan Fund, and went to places like Cairo and Zanzibar, consolidating what people thought would be a good direction for renovation projects, plus having a social and economic impact. We submitted our report in the summer of 1991 to His Highness, describing the opinions of those interviewed and proposing a design for the programme – which led to the specifications of the terms of reference, and to the hiring of Stefano Bianca.[60] I am very proud to have found him."[61] As Stefano Bianca in 2006 described his work: "Since its inception nearly fifteen years ago, the Historic Cities Support Programme has passed through various cycles of growth and development: first by implementing its three initial restoration/construction projects (Old Dispensary in Zanzibar, Baltit Fort in Hunza and Azhar Park in Cairo); then by expanding geographically (Samarkand, Mostar, Shigar, Delhi, Kabul and so on); and, most importantly, by expanding thematically, that is, by taking on board socio-economic development, institutional capacity-building and entrepreneurial initiatives that can help sustain cultural causes."[62] Luis Monreal, General Manager of the Aga Khan Trust for Culture, describes the Historic Cities Programme in other terms: "The point of the programme is to use cultural heritage to promote economic and social development in impoverished urban environments. The programme focuses on large areas of historic cities and not only addresses the need to restore or rehabilitate major historic buildings, but also works on public spaces, individual homes and urban infrastructure. It brings together the technical skills of architectural conservators, urban planners and development specialists, and promotes micro-finance initiatives, vocational training and health care. These projects create new, durable employment opportunities and help to form qualified people who subsequently work elsewhere as well. These initiatives have taken hold in Cairo in the Darb al-Ahmar district, in Kabul, in Lahore and more recently in the Nizamuddin area of Delhi, as well as in historic cities of the Sahel, such as Mopti or Timbuktu. The Historic Cities Programme works with the public sector, and its methodology and strategy is to set up public-private partnership agreements with corresponding public entities and other private partners. Collaboration between the public and private sectors is often a totally new experience in these places and it has proven to be a useful precedent."[63]

Some of the specific projects of the Historic Cities Programme are outlined elsewhere in this book, in particular the very large initiative to create Azhar Park in Cairo, to restore the neighbouring Ayyubid Wall and to revitalize the adjacent neighbourhood of al-Darb al-Ahmar. Luis Monreal points out that initiatives such as that undertaken by the Aga Khan in Afghanistan within a month of the end of the war there in December 2001 illustrate the new reactive capacities of the AKDN. "Investments such as those undertaken to create the Kabul Serena Hotel (see page 140) and the country's first mobile telephone network Roshan were coupled with a rural development programme spearheaded by the Aga Khan Fund, and such Historic Cities Programme initiatives as the rebuilding of the historic centres of Kabul and Herat, and the restoration of the Bagh-i Babur (Babur Gardens) and Timur Shah Mausoleum, projects which have already been completed."[64]

John de Monchaux, a very perceptive observer of the activities of the Aga Khan, gives a personal perspective on his former employer, in particular with reference to the origins of the Historic Cities Programme: "I had a chance to get a strong sense of His Highness's causes, of how he translated goals into operations. What is intriguing about the relationship of His Highness to the whole field of architecture is not just his innate sense about what good architecture is about, but an uncanny sense of the processes by which you achieve change in society, and using conviction to obtain consensus. And for operating in a way that lets the power of what others get done speak for the merit or worth of doing it. I mean that the discovery via a community in northern Pakistan or in Zanzibar or by an Award in Cairo – that self-discovery and recognition are the keys to the way the Aga Khan fosters excellence. He is able to place or insert his institutions into processes that are ongoing in communities or institutions and to do so in a way that the local objectives are not displaced, but their achievement is made much more certain. This capacity to act as a catalyst, as an inspirer, and to do it in a way that attends to the goals of the people is an inspired way to go about achieving change."[65]

The generosity and intelligence behind the Aga Khan Award for Architecture, the Historic Cities Programme, the Aga Khan Program for Islamic Architecture and, indeed, many of the other initiatives launched by the Aga Khan are firmly established. Assessing the degree of success of these efforts may be a somewhat more subjective process. Those most closely involved in the origins of the projects certainly have an informed viewpoint on these issues, but outside opinions are also of interest. Glenn Lowry is the Director of the Museum of Modern Art in New York and a member of the Steering Committee for the 2004 and 2007 Cycles of the Award. When asked how successful the Award has been, he responds: "In the academic and architectural communities the Award is taken very seriously. It is one of the few awards that looks at what was constructed and why, rather than who built it. It is admired for that. It has been around long enough and enough projects have received recognition for it to be well known and well respected within the professional world, but that does not mean it cannot be better known to the public, for example. The goal of the Award is a subtle goal, which is, over time, through recognition to stimulate a greater commitment on the part of clients in the Muslim world to make the effort to build better buildings and, conversely, to encourage architects to pay attention and take risks in order to create better buildings and for their efforts to be recognized. I do not know that the Award itself can or should do more than that. Of course, the Award's impact is always going to be diffuse and subtle, but I think over twenty-five years there is a much greater awareness about what it takes to build in the Islamic world. You cannot just take a plan designed for Paris or London and drop it in Jeddah and make a great building. You have to figure out what local conditions are – you have to pay attention. That does not mean every architect does that, but do the architects who are doing good buildings do it? Yes. A lot of the architects also use the Award research facility as they are planning projects."[66]

Above, a visit of
the site of the future
Azhar Park in Cairo,
Egypt, 1997.

Left, the Aga Khan
visiting the Old Stone
Town in Zanzibar,
Tanzania, in 1998.

When Nasser Rabbat, who is the Aga Khan Professor of Islamic Architecture at MIT, is asked if he feels that the Award has had a substantial impact in the Muslim world, he responds: "For the part of the Islamic world with which I am familiar, my answer is a resounding yes. I keep on meeting architects in Jordan, Syria, Egypt and Lebanon, the countries with which I am the most familiar … Every time that I say that I am the Aga Khan Professor of Islamic Architecture, they immediately start speaking about how their ultimate goal is to win an Aga Khan Award. I usually write about medieval architecture, but, in the past four or five years, I have been writing and giving lectures about contemporary architecture in the Arab world. I have been meeting more architects than I had in the past. Their reaction is almost always an expression of the hope or aspiration to receive the Aga Khan Award."[67]

Another of the current Aga Khan Professors, Gülru Necipoglu, affirms that the AKPIA Program at Harvard and MIT has had a substantial impact on Islamic studies in the United States. Of the Aga Khan, she says: "He is of course interested in architecture, but I believe he imagined it, in the context of the Aga Khan Program for Islamic Architecture, as a kind of mediation between the two worlds, which are not two opposite civilizations. He emphasized the living aspect of the culture instead of burying it in the medieval past. By funding these Programs, he has opened up the field. It used to be confined and esoteric. He emphasized the diversity, I think because of his own Ismaili faith – showing that there is not only one Islam. Until the 1970s there was a stereotyped vision of Islamic unity. It was viewed as being static. The emphasis on diversity made it a more real, connected study. The emphasis has gone from unity to diversity. Somehow there was only one connection to be made to Muslim civilizations – the medieval one. When you broaden it, you get the Chinese or African connections. This is not a rarefied esoteric world, but study has to do with context as well."[68] As one proof of the deep influence of the AKPIA Program, which is open to students from the Muslim world, Gülru Necipoglu cites an article published in *The Art Bulletin* by noted scholars, who write: "When we began studying Islamic art in the 1970s, we and our fellow students were virtually all white, non-Muslim Americans who had caught the Middle East 'bug'… This is not the case today. White non-Muslims are becoming less dominant in the field and many students are either Americanized descendants of Middle Eastern and Muslim immigrants … or Middle Eastern and Muslim students from abroad whose plans for the future are uncertain, given the frequent political storms that sweep through this troubled region. This new diversity of experience and expectation is welcome indeed, but it also raises complicated issues about who is doing what for whom."[69] This astonishing piece of prose is indeed a measure of the distance that has been travelled since the AKPIA was established, and perhaps also of the long road ahead. For Gülru Necipoglu the make-up of the student body in the Aga Khan Program at Harvard (about thirty-five per cent Muslim) is one element in the changes occurring in her field, while another is the openness inspired by the interaction of the studies of different topics and periods. She says: "The field is now studied in more diverse ways. In the old days, there were stereotypes that were easy to absorb. Part of the Aga Khan Program for Islamic Architecture was to make these studies more connected. All of a sudden the richness and diversity of Islamic history came to light. The medievalists held that around the tenth century a classical synthesis was formed and that everything after that was derivative and a less original form of expression."

Under the Eaves of Architecture

Given the very wide-ranging nature of the activities of the Aga Khan, such witnesses to the impact of his programmes can offer only a partial view in each case. And yet, the cumulative effect of these experiences is to confirm the character and inspiration of the Aga Khan himself, and his motivations and goals. On another front, that of the creation of Azhar Park in Cairo and its affiliated projects, Robert Ivy, the Editor in Chief of the respected American journal *Architectural Record*, states: "Looking at the work in Cairo, I frankly thought that that was an astounding event in the life of a city. It is something that would not have happened otherwise, and from that perspective it was quite extraordinary. Only a government with a will to invest to make such a gift to the urban place could have achieved something on this scale. It is an enlightened gift. It made something that otherwise would not have happened possible. As to the physical realization of the place, the more interesting aspect of it is the ancillary projects that spun off it, and these are typical of what the Aga Khan's building programmes have done. They are rarely monolithic activities; they tend to be multipartite. They tend to look at physical change in the context of the social environment and history, and, let us just say, in a variety of ways that most people do not. Most people do not have the interest or the capital or the entrepreneurial business interest to look at something and say how you can take this activity and make more out of it than if it were a solitary act. That is the most interesting component of the Park. The Park appears to be a beautiful addition to Cairo: the fact that the ancient wall was saved, that clinics were being set up in al-Darb al-Ahmar, that ancient mosques were being reclaimed, that there were social organizations, all of which were small things, is why I cite the entrepreneurial side of things. The act of giving seems to be tied with economic development and let us say a contextual, historic, urban fabric that is really probably singular. I do not know of any government or institutional entity that is achieving these sorts of things. It is a highly valued and quite wonderful opportunity. It is the kind of thing that an enlightened government should be doing, but that very few are able to achieve. They tend to be compromised for a variety of reasons, and these efforts tend not to be."[70]

When Robert Ivy speaks of looking "at physical change in the context of the social environment and history," he seems, indeed, to be approaching the essence of the fifty-year involvement of the Aga Khan in architecture. It appears clearly that where many patrons and clients of architecture see it as an end in itself, the Aga Khan is pursuing other goals, those of helping people to live better, of bringing them together to talk and to understand each other better. It is John de Monchaux who best sums up this unusual attitude: "When it comes to architecture there are two ways that I would describe his action. One is his eye for quality. It is an informed eye and it is also an instinctive one. The

The Aga Khan visiting the Old Stone Town of Zanzibar, Tanzania, in July 1991.

second is the phrase that he used in one of his speeches – 'under the eaves of architecture you can shelter a great many discussions.'[71] A great many topics can be debated under the shelter of architecture. Topics to do with human development or human rights, with urban opportunity, autonomy and accountability, things to do with ecology and sustainability. If you look at the chain of the Awards and the debates that were published in the books or the seminars you will get some sense of this incredible range of subjects which the eaves of architecture can shelter. I do not think that anyone has been brought under those eaves to debate under false pretences. It was a willing and interesting discussion that took place because architecture is a comfortable and accessible topic on which presidents of countries and leaders of the academic world and of the private sector all tend to have a view and are ready to be included in a debate that then touches on their responsibilities for the built environment. They were then confronted with the views that others had about their responsibilities. The exercise of those responsibilities in turn raised questions of respect, attention to the environment, sensitivity to cultural practice, and the understanding of legacies and history."[72]

Critics of architecture and those who follow the most contemporary developments in the field for whatever reason tend to isolate the formal or perhaps superficial aspects of new buildings. What do they look like? How 'original' are they? As a patron of architecture, in whatever context, the Aga Khan has always insisted on the comfort of users, and also on the relationship of a building to its location and its cultural context. More importantly still, he has created places for people to gather, to interact. Speaking of the Ismaili Centres built at the Aga Khan's instigation in numerous locations around the world, Dr Shafik Sachedina, Director of the Department of Diplomatic Affairs of the Ismaili Imamat, states clearly: "The notion of faith and the society in which you live are intertwined in Islam. There is no separation between what we call *din*, which is faith or the spiritual, and *dunya*, which is the world or the material. These are part and parcel while everyone lives the lives that they lead. You cannot have one without the other. You have to live that all the way through – in your work, in your interaction with people. Places of worship like this are not just for praying. There are seminars, plays, exhibitions, business meetings, and films or satellite football matches are shown – that is part of the world in which we live."[73]

The central importance of the concepts of *din* and *dunya* is outlined in the Ethical Framework established by the Institute of Ismaili Studies in London for the Aga Khan Development Network: "The institutions of the Aga Khan Development Network derive their impetus from the ethics of Islam which bridge the two realms of faith, *din* and *dunya*, the spiritual and the material. The central emphasis of Islam's ethical ideal is enablement of each person to live up to his exalted status as vicegerent of God on earth, in whom God has breathed His own spirit and to whom He has made whatever is in the heavens and the earth an object of trust and quest. A person's ultimate worth depends on how he or she responds to these Divine favours. *Din* is the spiritual relationship of willing submission of a reasoning creature to his Lord, who creates, sustains and guides. The earthly life, *dunya*, is a gift to cherish inasmuch as it is a bridge to, and preparation for, the life to come … Service of God is not only worship, but also service to humanity, and abiding by the duty of trust toward the rest of creation. Righteousness, says the Koran, is not only fulfilling one's religious obligations. Without social responsibility, religiosity is a show of conceit. Islam is, therefore, both *din* and *dunya*, spirit and matter, distinct, but linked, neither to be forsaken."[74] The point is undoubtedly that these thoughts underlie not only the Ismaili Centres, but are at the very heart of the engagement of the Aga Khan with the physical environment and the "processes of change." Each initiative expresses these ideas anew but remains profoundly rooted in the role of the Imam, but also of the man, confronted with an extraordinary destiny and an unparalleled capacity to assist others.

This is not to say that the positions of the Aga Khan have been set in stone from the first, indeed, his method is much more clearly one of embracing change and encouraging it. The organizations that he has created have been shown to spring from his own questions, but also from the efforts of those he has assembled around him. The Aga Khan gave the 1994 Commencement Speech at the Massachusetts Institute of Technology in which he said: "I shall talk today about encounters. Encounters. When two people meet. Or two particles. Or two cultures. In that crucial moment of interaction the results of an encounter are determined. In the simplest of encounters – say, with two billiard balls – the outcome is a predictable result of position, velocity and mass. But the encounters that interest me most are not so simple. In the encounters of people and cultures, much depends on the path that each has taken to that point. These are not stochastic processes. The subjects have histories. The encounter has complexity and rich dimensionality. The result of an encounter between two people or between two cultures is shaped by the assumptions of each, by their respective goals and – perhaps most directly relevant to a university – by the repertoire of responses that each has learned. Encounters therefore have aspects of both the general and the specific. What makes our current time distinctive are the new combinations of people and cultures that are participating in these encounters."[75] Once more, it is apparent that he considers architecture to be a means rather than an end, a way to bring people together, and to emphasize the durable traditions of the Muslim and developing world.

Canada and the Road to Pluralism

One fascinating example of the evolving plans and programmes of the Aga Khan is the number of substantial architectural projects he has undertaken in recent years in Canada. When he became Imam in 1957, the Ismaili population of Canada was very small. Events elsewhere in the world changed that. Firoz Rasul, who was President of the Aga Khan Council for Canada for six years and led the development of various high-level projects for the Aga Khan Development Network, including the future Global Centre for Pluralism and the Aga Khan Museum in Toronto, is now President of the Aga Khan University in Karachi. He points out that the precise size of the Ismaili population in the country is not known. "We do not have an exact number but I would say that it is between sixty and seventy-five thousand. The first Ismailis began arriving in the early 1970s from Uganda and Tanzania. Thirty years have now passed and I think that the resettlement has gone reasonably well."[76] The first substantial project of the Imamat in Canada was the Ismaili Centre and Jamatkhana in Burnaby (British Columbia).[77] More recently plans were announced to create a building for the Delegation of the Ismaili Imamat in Ottawa, a Centre for Global Pluralism in the same city, the Aga Khan Museum in Toronto and an Ismaili Centre and Jamatkhana on the same site in Toronto.

In terms of the ongoing activities of the Aga Khan, it may be that the most significant of these initiatives is the Global Centre for Pluralism. To be housed in the former Canadian War Museum in Ottawa, the Centre will seek to "produce, collect and disseminate applicable knowledge and know-how about the values, policies and practices that underpin pluralist societies."[78] When the Aga Khan announced this project, he declared: "In my own role as Imam of the Shia Ismaili Muslims over the past half century, I have come to appreciate the importance of pluralism in ever-expanding ways. The Ismaili community, after all, is itself a global family, spanning many geographies, cultures, languages and ethnicities – and sharing its life with people of many faiths. In addition, much of my work over this time has dealt with highly diverse societies in the developing world, often suffering from poverty, violence and despair. In such circumstances, a commitment to pluralism comes as no accident. For pluralism, in essence, is a deliberate set of choices that a society must make if it is to avoid costly conflict and harness the power of its diversity in solving human problems."[79] The government of Canada and the Aga Khan have contributed equal, large sums toward the endowment of this institution. The 3800-square-metre building, located at 330 Sussex Drive, is a well-known historic landmark on what is also known as Canada's Confederation Boulevard. Erected between 1904 and 1925,[80] it served first as the Dominion Archives (1904–67) and then as the War Museum (1968–2005). The location of this and other projects launched by the Aga Khan in Canada is based not only on the presence of an Ismaili population but also on his own observations of the

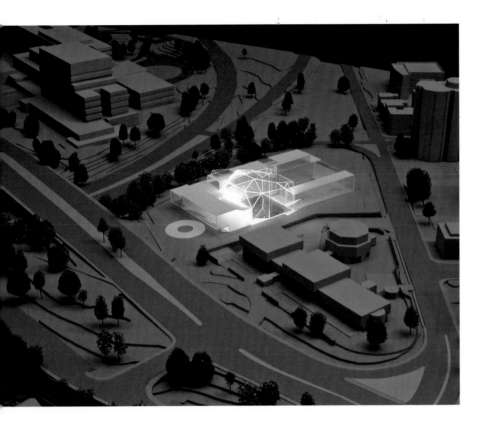

A model of the Delegation of the Ismaili Imamat. Presently under construction in Ottawa, Canada, the building was designed by the Japanese architect Fumihiko Maki.

country. "It will not surprise you," he declared, "that I am fascinated by Canada's experience as a successful pluralistic society. My active engagement with Canada began in the 1970s when many Ismailis found a welcoming refuge here in Canada from East African ethnic strife. Since that time, the Ismaili community has planted deep roots here, become self-sufficient, and can now make its own contributions to Canada's pluralistic model. That model, in turn, is one which can help to teach and inspire the entire world." With sensitivity to Canada's bilingual tradition, the Aga Khan continued this speech in French: "Comme les Canadiens le savent si bien, l'idéal du pluralisme n'est pas nouveau en ce monde. Il a des fondations honorables et anciennes, y compris des racines profondes dans la tradition islamique. Ce qui est sans précédent aujourd'hui, c'est une société mondialisée, intimement interconnectée et extraordinairement interdépendante."[81]

Some might ask what this initiative has to do with architecture other than the announced restoration of a historic building. In fact, the Global Centre for Pluralism has everything to do with the approach of the Aga Khan to architecture as an element in the processes of change of which he speaks. It is not an accident that he spoke of the "honourable and ancient foundations" of pluralism. This is an architecture of the mind and of the soul, the architecture that is truly the one that has inhabited the Aga Khan for fifty years and more. "Tolerance, openness and understanding toward other peoples' cultures, social structures, values and faiths are now essential to the very survival of an interdependent world," he said. "Pluralism is no longer simply an asset or a prerequisite for progress and development, it is vital to our existence."[82]

Architecture in a somewhat more traditional sense is the object of the Aga Khan's choice of the noted Japanese architect Fumihiko Maki to build the Delegation of the Ismaili Imamat in Ottawa, also on Sussex Drive, and the Aga Khan Museum on a site to include a new Ismaili Centre and Jamatkhana by Charles Correa in Toronto. Although the Museum was still in the process of design as this book went to press, the relationship of the Aga Khan to the architect provides a different insight into his involvement in the art of building. In a letter addressed to Fumihiko Maki on 3 January 2006, the Aga Khan refers to his hope that light will suffuse the new building. He writes of "two notions related to the sources of Light: The first source is natural light emanating from God's creation …

The second area of symbolism in the notion of 'Light' is that which emanates from human sources, in the form of art, culture and well-inspired human knowledge."[83] Shams Vellani of the Institute of Ismaili Studies in London explains: "His Highness has laid out the relations between past, present and future, and to the very clear mystical or esoteric tradition in Islam. His speeches also address the question of the strengthening of faith and the world, *din* and *dunya* in Islam. This explains why a spiritual leader is involved with things that might be considered mundane, such as architecture, rural development, social and economic development." Indeed, as the Aga Khan himself says in the interview that follows this text, the spiritual can be found in many places. The light of which he speaks in the future Aga Khan Museum in Toronto is obviously a manifestation of this spirituality.

Protecting the Past and Inspiring the Future

Bringing together the thoughts and lessons of more than a quarter century of activity, the Aga Khan gave a speech at the Ninth Award Cycle ceremony in Delhi in 2004. He first explained the situation that had motivated his creation of the Award: "In recent years, Islamic architecture seemed to have lost its identity – I should perhaps say identities – and its inspiration. Occasionally, construction tended to repeat previous Islamic styles, but much more often, it simply absorbed imported architectural forms, language and materials … There were several reasons for this. In part, it was because 'modernity,' equated with all that was Western, had come to be seen as representing improved quality. And most Muslim architects were trained in Western schools and had little knowledge and understanding of the traditions of Islamic architecture … The net result was that our cities, villages and rural areas were being transformed by the insidious introduction and expansion of inappropriate and irrelevant archi-

A view at dusk in the Darb al-Ahmar area of Cairo, Egypt, with the restored Khayrbek Mausoleum and Minaret on the left.

tecture and planning." From this analysis of a deplorable situation, he first defines his own responsibility and that of others: "In Islam, the Holy Koran says that man is God's noblest creation to whom He has entrusted the stewardship of all that is on earth. Each generation must leave for its successors an enhanced and sustainable social and physical environment. I am sure every responsible citizen in every part of the world would share this aspiration." With this affirmation at heart, he says: "We set out on a long journey to try to understand the causes of this sad situation which Muslim and non-Muslim architects alike recognized as unfortunate, but which none knew how to alter. They included some of the most eminent architects, and men and women of different disciplines and cultures who joined me in this endeavour to understand the causes of this decline in quality and design." The Aga Khan's own perception of the Award and surely of his other efforts is that a great deal may still be accomplished, and yet, as he says: "Our efforts have been richly rewarded in the growth of knowledge and awareness of Islamic architecture and landscaping in educational bodies around the world. In the most eminent Western schools there is a much greater academic offering and commitment to the field of Islamic architecture … and in Muslim countries we have seen the birth of new schools and a new generation of architectural teachers and scholars in the field. Most important, as we have seen from the winners recognized this evening, we are getting better habitat. I think that the Award and the cluster of initiatives born from it are truly protecting the past and inspiring the future."[84]

A certain number of specific examples of the projects selected by the Aga Khan Award over the years and a number of the projects his organizations have undertaken in the area of architecture are published in the pages that follow this essay and an interview given in London in March 2007. Despite the wide range of these projects, from the restoration of historic buildings to the most contemporary architecture, it is difficult to give a full picture of the activities of the Aga Khan over the fifty years of his Imamat. The topic chosen for this book, his involvement in architecture, indeed opens a window onto his proactive engagement with the processes of change. It is no exaggeration to say that few individuals have contributed so much to the improvement of the physical environment of so many. So, too, few have done as much to make the truth of Islam apparent, to build bridges between worlds, between Islam and the West, between the poor and those who have the means to help them. As His Highness the Aga Khan concluded in his 2004 speech in Delhi: "Perhaps these lessons will one day be seen as an important contribution from the Muslim world: a contribution to the broader cause of maintaining and enhancing a multicultural, pluralist world and a responsive, appropriate human habitat."[85]

The French philosopher Michel Serres concludes his remarkable book 'The Art of Bridges – Homo Pontifex'[86] with the following soliloquy: "Ni *Homo pontifex*[86] ni quelque pontife n'ont à chercher, à desirer ni à occuper de places hiérarchiques; il les refuseraient plutôt, tout occupés à construire des ponts vers les autres ou à les acceuillur sur leur rive. Les autres nous sauvent selon l'amour que nous leur portons. Si je n'ai pas la charité, je puis parler cent langues, mais je n'en dirai pas plus que l'airain sonnant d'une cymbale qu'un gong fait retentir. La charité tolère tout, croit tout, espère et souffre tout. Elle ouvre le pont universel."[87]

1 The all-embracing Islamic community.

2 Koran 2:164; 3:190–191; 30:22 ff.; 51:20–21. Quotation from http://www.akdn.org/imamat/imamat.html.

3 See: http://www.akdn.org/imamat/imamat.html.

4 In 969 the Fatimids entered Fustat with little resistance: Jawhar al-Siqili founded al-Qahira in anticipation of the arrival of the Fatimid Imam/Caliph al-Muizz from North Africa. Al-Qahira then became the seat of the Fatimid empire. See: http://www.akdn.org/hcsp/Cairo1_13.pdf.

5 See: http://www.akdn.org/imamat/imamat.html.

6 W. Somerset Maugham, 'Forward', in: *The Memoirs of Aga Khan*, London 1954.

7 Ibid.

8 'Aly Khan's Son, 20, New Aga Khan', in: *The New York Times*, 13 July 1957.

9 *Ismaili Mirror*, February 1971.

10 See: http://www.akdn.org/imamat/imamat.html.

11 Ibid.

12 Ibid.

13 See: http://www.akdn.org/about.html.

14 Aga Khan Agency for Microfinance (AKAM); Aga Khan Foundation (AKF); Aga Khan Education Services (AKES); Aga Khan Fund for Economic Development (AKFED); Aga Khan Health Services (AKHS); Aga Khan Planning and Building Services (AKPBS); Aga Khan Trust for Culture (AKTC); Aga Khan University (AKU); University of Central Asia (UCA).

15 See: http://www.akdn.org/agency/aktc.html.

16 Address by His Highness the Aga Khan, Foundation Ceremony of the Delegation of the Ismaili Imamat, Ottawa, Canada, 6 June 2005. See: http://www.akdn.org/speeches/2005June6.html.

17 In 1958, the capital of Pakistan was shifted from Karachi to Rawalpindi, and then to Islamabad in 1960.

18 On 10 September 1958, the Aga Khan officially opened the Aga Khan Platinum Jubilee Hospital in Nairobi, Kenya.

19 Interview with Gerald Wilkinson, Menaggio, Italy, 17 August 2006.

20 Ibid.

21 Interview with Don Olson, Geneva, Switzerland, 3 June 2006.

22 Morgan Dix Wheelock attended Harvard University's Graduate School of Design and has a Master of Landscape Architecture. He was associated for fourteen years with the office of Sasaki Associates Inc. in Watertown, Massachusetts. He became a Principal of Sasaki Associates in 1969, and for eight years was Vice President of the company and Principal in charge of all international projects. During this time he developed for Sasaki Associates its international reputation in the field of tourism and recreational development. In order to develop a smaller professional office through which a deeper and more constant involvement of his own time in each project would be achieved, he founded Morgan Wheelock Incorporated in 1978. Today, in addition to his numerous affiliations, trusteeships, memberships and fellowships, he holds the position of Chairman of the Town of Palm Beach Architectural Commission and remains Principal and President of Morgan Wheelock Incorporated.

23 Interview with Don Olson, Geneva, Switzerland, 3 June 2006.

24 Bruno Foucart, *Pierre Barbe, Architectures*, Liège 1991.

25 Interview in writing with Garr Campbell, 9 January 2007.

26 Ibid.

27 The roots of the company extend back to 1932 when the firm was called Markus and Nocka and focused on industrial design for the improvement of health-care facilities. In 1960, Tom Payette joined the firm which became Payette Associates Inc. in 1974, after Markus and Nocka retired. Under Tom Payette's energetic and inspirational leadership, the practice grew to include a broad base of clients in colleges, universities, schools of medicine and corporations. In 1998, Payette completed a successful transition of leadership and ownership. James H. Collins Jr was elected President and the Principals of the firm took on a more equal participation. These changes in leadership have brought new energy and focus to the firm. Today, the firm is comprised of approximately 140 people and has a global practice. It is organized as three highly collaborative design studios and supported by in-house expertise in interior design and landscape architecture.

28 Interview with Tom Payette, Boston, 3 November 2006.

29 Ibid.

30 Ibid.

31 William Lyman Porter was Dean of MIT's School of Architecture and Planning (1971–81) and then Head of the Department of Architecture (1987–91).

32 His Highness the Aga Khan, Welcome Address at the First Seminar of the Aga Khan Award for Architecture, Aiglemont, France, April 1978.

33 Ibid.

34 See: http://www.akdn.org/agency/aktc_akaa.html#intro.

35 Oleg Grabar, currently Professor Emeritus at the Institute for Advanced Study in the School of Historical Studies (Princeton, New Jersey). His research has had a profound and far-reaching influence on the study of Islamic art and architecture. He served as a Professor at Harvard beginning in 1969, and as the first Aga Khan Professor of Islamic Art and Architecture when that chair was established at Harvard in 1980.

36 Architect of the Ismaili Centre and Jamatkhana, London, 1981. Sir Hugh Casson (1910–99) was director of architecture at the 1951 Festival of Britain on London's South Bank. He was Provost of the Royal College of Art (1970), then President of the Royal Academy (1976–84). As a member of the first two Steering Committees for the Aga Khan Award for Architecture (1980, 1983) Hugh Casson had a significant influence on the creation and early directions of the Award.

37 Nader Ardalan is an Iranian architect. He writes: "I believe that good architecture should reflect a holistic appreciation of reality. Reality, it is held, has a hierarchy of awareness levels within which there exists both outer and inner dimensions. The outer (ecological) dimension relates to a finite world of limited energy-income from the sun, of fixed energy reserves. The inner (cultural) dimension relates to humankind, who have an infinite, hidden reserve of energy – the spirit – that can often transcend the limited context of this phenomenal world." See: http://archnet.org.

38 Egyptian architect (1899–1989) who devoted himself to housing the poor in developing nations. See: http://archnet.org for more information.

39 Interview with Oleg Grabar, Princeton, New Jersey, 30 October 2006.

40 Interview with William Porter, MIT, Cambridge, Massachusetts, 3 November 2006.

41 Renata Holod has been a Professor in the Department of the History of Art at the University of Pennsylvania since 1993. She was Chair of the Department from 1987 to 1994 and from 2000 to 2002.

42 Interview with Renata Holod, Geneva, Switzerland, 23 March 2006.

43 Ibid.

44 *Mimar: Architecture in Development* was a magazine first published by the Aga Khan in 1981. In its forty-three issues, it focused on countries seeking "new directions for their built environment." All forty-three issues of Mimar are available in the Digital Library at http://archnet.org.

45 Interview with Hasan Uddin Khan, Concorde, Massachusetts, 2 November 2006.

46 Ibid.

47 Ibid.

48 Emilio Ambasz was born in 1943 in Argentina and studied at Princeton University. He is a highly reputed designer and architect. He served as Curator of Design at the Museum of Modern Art in New York (1970–76).

49 Interview with Hasan Uddin Khan, Concorde, Massachusetts, 2 November 2006.

50 Unpublished interview with His Highness the Aga Khan by Oleg Grabar, Boston, 1998.

51 His Highness the Aga Khan, Presentation Ceremony of the Aga Khan Award for Architecture, Lahore, Pakistan, 23 October 1980.

52 Ibid.

53 Balkrishna Vithaldas Doshi was born in Poona, India, in 1927. After he completed his studies at J. J. School of Art, Bombay, in 1950 he became a senior designer on Le Corbusier's projects in Ahmedabad and Chandigarh. In 1956 he established a

private practice in Vastu-Shilpa, Ahmedabad, and in 1962 he established the Vastu-Shilpa Foundation for Environmental Design. He also founded and designed the School of Architecture and Planning in Ahmedabad. Doshi has worked in partnership as Stein, Doshi & Bhalla since 1977. Over the years Doshi has created architecture that relies on a sensitive adoption and refinement of modern architecture within an Indian context. The relevancy of his environmental and urban concerns makes him unique as both a thinker and a teacher. Architectural scale and massing, as well as a clear sense of space and community, mark most of his work. Doshi's architecture provides one of the most important models for modern Indian architecture.

54 Interview with William Porter, MIT, Cambridge, Massachusetts, 3 November 2006.

55 Derek Bok was President of Harvard University from 1971 to 1991 and again in 2006–07.

56 Jerome Wiesner (1915–94) was President of the Massachusetts Institute of Technology (MIT) from 1971 to 1980.

57 Interview with Oleg Grabar, Princeton, New Jersey, 30 October 2006.

58 Interview with His Highness the Aga Khan by Robert Ivy, Editor in Chief, *Architectural Record*, Aiglemont, France, 31 August 2001. See: http://www.akdn.org/agency/akaa/eighthcycle/intrvue.htm.

59 John de Monchaux is Professor of Architecture and Urban Planning at MIT. He was Dean of the School of Architecture and Planning (1981–92) and served as General Manager of the Aga Khan Trust for Culture in Geneva, Switzerland (1992–96).

60 Stefano Bianca was Director of the Historic Cities Support Programme (now the Historic Cities Programme) from 1992 to 2006.

61 Interview with John de Monchaux, MIT, Cambridge, Massachusetts, 2 November 2006.

62 Stefano Bianca, 'HCSP Development Review Paper', Geneva, Switzerland, 20 April 2006.

63 Interview with Luis Monreal, Geneva, Switzerland, 28 March 2007.

64 Ibid.

65 Interview with John de Monchaux, MIT, Cambridge, Massachusetts, 2 November 2006.

66 Interview with Glenn Lowry, Paris, France, 12 July 2006.

67 Interview with Nasser Rabbat, MIT, Cambridge, Massachusetts, 1 November 2006.

68 Interview with Gülru Necipoglu, Harvard, Cambridge, Massachusetts, 2 November 2006.

69 Sheila S. Blair and Jonathan M. Bloom, 'The Mirage of Islamic Art: Reflections on the Study of an Unwieldy Field', in: *The Art Bulletin*, March 2003, Volume LXXXV, Number 1. *The Art Bulletin* is a quarterly published by the College Art Association.

70 Interview with Robert Ivy, Editor in Chief, *Architectural Record*, New York, 7 November 2006.

71 John de Monchaux recalls that this phrase was included in a draft of a speech he prepared for the Aga Khan at the American Institute of Architects (AIA) convention in 1992. "The phrase itself may not have found its way into the speech as delivered but I do have a recollection of discussing the idea with the Aga Khan and of his ready acknowledgment that it captured both the direct and the more subtle aspects of his intent. As with many aphorisms that may begin life in discussions about architecture, such as 'less is more', 'God is in the details', the original source of the metaphor, as I have used it, may forever remain unremembered. I certainly think of the activities of the AKTC, the AKF, the Housing Boards, the Aga Khan Universities and their design, and so on, as all sheltering fresh and critical discourse about many issues well outside the ordinary realm of architectural commentary." E-mail from John de Monchaux, 27 March 2007.

72 Interview with John de Monchaux, MIT, Cambridge, Massachusetts, 2 November 2006.

73 Interview with Dr Shafik Sachedina, Aiglemont, Gouvieux, France, 13 September 2006.

74 Aga Khan Development Network (AKDN), 'An Ethical Framework Prepared for the Aga Khan Development Network by the Institute of Ismaili Studies', February 2000. See: http://www.iis.ac.uk/view_article.asp?ContentID=101094.

75 His Highness the Aga Khan, Commencement Speech at the Massachusetts Institute of Technology, 27 May 1994. See: http://www.akdn.org/speeches/mit_94.html.

76 Interview with Firoz Rasul, Geneva, Switzerland, 31 May 2006.

77 Architect/Planner: Bruno Freschi, 1984.

78 'Using the Former Canadian War Museum to Its Full Potential: The Global Centre for Pluralism', Global Centre for Pluralism press release, 18 October 2006.

79 His Highness the Aga Khan, speech on the occasion of the signing of the Funding Agreement for the Global Centre for Pluralism, Ottawa, Canada, 25 October 2006.

80 Original architects Band, Burritt, Meredith and Ewart, who designed several other government buildings of the period.

81 His Highness the Aga Khan, speech on the occasion of the signing of the Funding Agreement for the Global Centre for Pluralism, Ottawa, Canada, 25 October 2006. "As Canadians know so well, the idea of pluralism is not a new one in this world. It has honourable and ancient foundations, including deep roots in Islamic tradition. What is new, today, is that society is globalized, intimately interconnected and extraordinarily interdependent."

82 'Aga Khan Welcomes Government of Canada's Partnership in New Global Centre for Pluralism', press release, Ottawa, Canada, 18 April 2005. See: http://www.akdn.org/news/2005April18.htm.

83 His Highness the Aga Khan, unpublished letter to Professor Fumihiko Maki, Aiglemont, France, 3 January 2006.

84 His Highness the Aga Khan, speech at the Ninth Award Cycle of the Aga Khan Award for Architecture, New Delhi, India, 27 November 2004. See: http://www.akdn.org/speeches/Speech_AKAA2004.htm.

85 Ibid.

86 The word pontiff comes from the Latin word *pontifex*, which was the title of certain Roman high priests. It can mean bridge-maker, from the Latin *ponti-* (*pons*, bridge) and *fex* (from *facere*, to do or to make).

87 Michel Serres, *L'art des ponts – Homo pontifex*, Paris 2006. "Neither *Homo pontifex* nor any pontiff need search, desire or occupy hierarchical spaces; they would rather refuse them, since they are so occupied building bridges toward others, or busy greeting those who have crossed to their shore. Others save us according to the love that we bring them. If I do not have charity, I could speak one hundred languages, but I would not be able to say more than the ringing iron of a cymbal struck by a gong. Charity tolerates all, believes all, hopes and suffers all. It opens the universal bridge."

THE PROCESSES OF CHANGE

His Highness the Aga Khan: I will be talking about things that I have not talked about before. Your questions prompted me to think back to what the situation was when I became the Imam in 1957. The first ten years of Imamat caused me to become more and more involved in what you call architecture and what I would call the processes of change.

PJ: Is it true that you had originally considered studying architecture or engineering?

His Highness the Aga Khan: No, neither architecture nor engineering specifically. My grandfather had wanted me to study the sciences, because at that time he felt that the Islamic world did not participate in the development of modern science. The history of the Islamic world, on the contrary, had been meshed with the environment of science and astronomy, medicine and so many different fields. I did all of my secondary school with the intent of going into the sciences. In fact, I applied first to the Massachusetts Institute of Technology (MIT) because that was the normal destiny for a student who wanted to specialize in the sciences at the time. I was admitted to MIT, but then when I met up with my grandfather before going to university, he said: "I think that the sciences field is too narrow, therefore I would like you to go to Harvard." I had to backtrack on my education up until then, including language, because Harvard had much more rigorous English-language requirements than MIT did. I had done most of my education in French at the time. I did apply to Harvard, and in the first years there I spent a lot of time in the sciences. At the end of my sophomore year, I decided to move into history. I did my junior year and whatever was left of my senior year in history.

PJ: In the history of Islam?

His Highness the Aga Khan: Yes.

PJ: At that time, did you have a specific interest in the architecture of Islam?

His Highness the Aga Khan: No. It was the general field of Islamic studies. Yes, you learned about the great buildings of the Islamic world, the great names in history and philosophy, the empires of the Islamic world, the languages and the people. You would not have reached a very intense degree of specificity unless you had been doing an M.A. or a Ph.D., which is what I hoped to do, but of course my grandfather died before I was even able to complete my undergraduate studies.

PJ: What are some of the ways in which you came to be interested in architecture early in your Imamat?

His Highness the Aga Khan: I have thought about your question and it brings me back to what happened between 1957 and 1967. I travelled extensively, meeting with various communities in different parts of the world. I came into contact with visible forms of poverty that I had not known before. I had been educated in Switzerland and the United States. Anyone who visited the slums of Karachi in 1957, or who visited the high mountain areas in the Karakoram,[1] or who simply visited the periphery of Bombay or Calcutta, came into direct physical contact with levels of poverty which were absolutely indescribable, and which were very much evidenced by the physical environment in which the people lived. The first indicator of a community's poverty, what you see, is the physical context in which they live. Therefore, my interest in architecture was driven at that time by the question of what to do to improve the quality of life of the ultra-poor. That brought into focus a very serious question that impacted my thinking on architecture. It was apparent that the material needs to change this process were so enormous that the idea that these parts of the world could ever enter the domain of the consumer society was simply unrealistic. What you were doing at the time was to look at every way possible to obtain the highest return on any investment, whether it was for a school or a hospital, or housing. It was not possible to think in terms of the useful life of a building. The useful life of a building was quite simply as long as it was going to

stand up. That completely changed my attitude to building programmes. Whereas in the consumer societies of the West you can build and then pull things down, in these ultra-poor societies you cannot afford to do that. What you have to do is to modify buildings or adjust them; therefore, the flexibility of the plan that you put in place has to be conceived with a different view of time than it would be in other parts of the world. If you think about it, this is self-evident. Architecture is the only art that is a direct reflector of poverty. Music does not reflect poverty in a tactile way, nor does literature. In architecture

there is an inherent and unavoidable demonstration of the quality of life, or its absence. At that time, I was looking at how to deal with these situations. I inherited projects that my grandfather had started, or that the communities had started. There were schools that were under construction, there was the Aga Khan Platinum Jubilee Hospital in Nairobi, and there were various other projects as well. My grandfather was vigorously involved in the field of housing, particularly in East Africa, but also elsewhere. He set up some very fine housing organizations.

Obviously these were programmes that were running and, therefore, what I was concerned about at the time was, in particular, completing institutional buildings. Every time that problem was on the table, the issue was fairly simple; you either had an opportunity to change or modify, or you did not. Where projects were not frozen or where new initiatives were necessary, change was possible. The question was, if you can change, should you? And what change would you make? Then, if you were building a new programme, the question was, are you building the right programme? Are you building flexibility into that programme? Because at that stage it was clearly necessary. What is the idiom that you build in? Do you build using the language of the West, which is what the situation was at the time, wherever you built? It had become the omnipresent language of architecture and was even called the International Style. You ended up with schools or medical centres all over the developing world, in Africa or Asia, which all came back to this basic language of architecture. Two things came into focus at that time. One was the need to think through building programmes much more intensely than had been the case before because of the awareness of resource limitations, and the need to be able to modify buildings if that was necessary. The second issue was the actual architectural language that you used, but at the time there was no alternative. The only architects who were practising that I came into contact with in Africa or Asia from 1957, for at least ten years or more, were people who had been exclusively educated in Western schools of architecture, who might have had an academic interest in inherited architecture, but an academic interest only. There was no endeavour to revive the architectural languages of other cultures. At a later date, I asked myself whether this direction, which was in a sense an imposed direction, or a consensus of the time, was in fact the right one. I came to the conclusion that that was the question that had to be asked of a very wide spectrum of thinkers in the Islamic world and beyond. That was, of course, the essence of the Award for Architecture. The moment that question was asked, this whole spectrum of issues was on the table.

PJ: When you make reference to hospitals and schools, were these for the benefit of the Ismaili community?

His Highness the Aga Khan: They were not at the time. The schools in 1957 were mixed schools. The Aga Khan Hospital in Nairobi was the first multi-community hospital in Kenya. Before that, all of the hospitals were African, European or Asian.

PJ: You speak of the need for flexibility. Is that something that you began to impose very quickly on the constructions that you were involved in?

His Highness the Aga Khan: The difficulty was to try to understand what were the hypothetical directions that you could go in. If you built a general hospital in 1958, what was going to happen to that hospital twenty or thirty years later? Some things were predictable, some were not. What was predictable was the need to grow. What was much less predictable, at least for me at the time, was the nature of change in medicine. Today, the nature of medicine has changed enormously. The duration of hospitalization was not a factor that was taken into account extensively in 1957, so you tended to get all sorts of cases: for example, some people were incurably ill, but were still hospital-based. Where surgery was concerned, hospitalization was often for a week or ten days at a time, whereas today a lot of that is done on a day basis. That has changed the nature of the programmes of hospitals. Day care is much more prominent than it was fifty years ago. The nature of change in medicine, but also in education, was not predictable, but rising demand was. What was done was to leave extra land and to place technical facilities so that you could extend when you needed to extend.

PJ: You became involved very early in the actual art of architecture and construction, and you went to visit the sites. You then started to change the direction of construction…

His Highness the Aga Khan: I watched and I asked questions, because the Imamat was responsible for much of this building and the community would identify needs and put forward requests for a school or a medical centre. Yes, I obviously went to see what was actually happening, to try to understand what we were doing. Being directly involved in these situations, you learn about poverty by going to see the way people live and

Taken in 1960, this photo shows the Aga Khan with a model of the Costa Smeralda development, and the actual site in the background.

by talking to the ultra-poor. You do not learn it from books.

PJ: From a later period onwards, that of the Award, you have had contact with very well-known architects. Were there any individuals who had a real influence on your approach to architecture? If you had to select one building that has most influenced you, which one would it be?

His Highness the Aga Khan: I would not be able to recall specific names, but those who were strong in what I would call "programmatic" buildings, in medical or educational architecture, were my partners. It is not that I worked with them intimately, because, frankly, there were just too many projects going on. A lot of them were "colonial" practices. As for the buildings that have had an impact on me, there is one that I would give as an example, the Ahmad Ibn Tulun Mosque in Cairo, where I think that the interrelationship between space and building is just extraordinary. It is incredibly simple, but you cannot walk into a more remarkable space.

PJ: The notion of space you refer to is not necessarily only ancient, it could be modern as well.

His Highness the Aga Khan: Absolutely.

PJ: Do you make a clear distinction between the creation of the Costa Smeralda resort in Sardinia, for example, and the architecture you were involved with as Imam?

His Highness the Aga Khan: In a sense yes, in a sense no. If it is a private initiative, you are looking at the eco-

nomic factor more than you might be doing elsewhere. If you build a school or a hospital, at least in the case of our activities, they are non-profit institutions. While we try more and more to balance the situation so that we do not create an increasing number of loss operations in health care and education, the buildings were not conceived to generate maximum income in order to create a profit. There is a commonality between the two. I have always tried to look at the context in which a building was occurring. Personally, I am uncomfortable with what I would call decontextualization. I feel uncomfortable if an architect wilfully seeks a conflict with the environment. I feel that that is not appropriate. In Sardinia, we had an unusual situation in that there was no building. The only people in the area were shepherds, who cared for their flocks during the summer in sheds which were empty in the winter. It was a total green-field site. One of the driving factors in the environment was its lack of scale. It was a geophysical area where everything was small. The mountains, the vegetation, even the people were small. If you had gone into that environment with high-rise buildings, you would have created an absolute catastrophe. People talk about the architecture there, but it is much more a question of the management of scale than of the quality of the architectural designs. We started by looking for what was traditional in the region. The basic premise of the Costa Smeralda was quite interesting, and it has become a case study in a number of schools I think. You have a green-field site, and most developers will go into a site like that and they will say: "How do I optimize my return? I do not care what happens to the site, to the seafront, to the vegetation, I am going to put the maximum density in for the highest return." We did exactly the opposite. We started with the land planners, which was not the normal order of things at the time. We had them analyse the site, which was a complex task because there were no roads. It was a difficult site even to walk through because of the vegetation. There were no contour maps, we had no working documents. We were able to do the survey and to determine what were the driving parts of the area. If you altered these, you affected the visual impact of the whole area. These were the higher mountain areas, the promontories coming out into the ocean. Once we had done the planning, the next question was: "Is it economic?" That is when the economists came in and studied the land plans; they looked at the

buildability of each type of activity, and their answer was: "Yes, it can be an economically viable venture." There were so many conditions, such as access, which was a major problem. There was an absence of normal leisure area facilities, medical facilities, infrastructure, the need for water, the fact that there was no commerce and therefore no access to food or household goods. We started from absolute zero. Even the city that we were leaning on, which was Olbia, was not a leisure city.

What was done there was very different from the institutional work that I was doing in the 1950s and 1960s, but in the mid 1960s the question of the nature of economic change in the developing world came up. What are the forces that can come into play to diversify national economies, to create foreign exchange income, to create more employment? One response was the leisure industry. I had created an agency that was at first called IPS, the Industrial Promotion Services. There the premise was that you wanted to develop new entrepreneurship, but away from commerce and into the high levels of production. We started in the industrial field, but very soon it became apparent, in East Africa for example, that the leisure industry was going to be a powerful driver of economic change, if it was developed properly. That is where the Sardinia experience came to be very significant because we had developed the knowledge about how to create a leisure industry from nothing. We had the professional partners that we needed, the land analysts, the economists, we had some human resources that we could rely on. What came out of a private sector engagement in the leisure field has been folded back into the development of these countries, and that is why we were one of the first organizations to get seriously involved in the leisure industry in East Africa. A lot of the environmental and architectural thinking that you see today in the leisure field was in a sense created or learnt about in Sardinia.

PJ: Your own interest in landscape design has been expressed on many occasions. Does that interest also come from Sardinia?

His Highness the Aga Khan: No. Landscape design really came to me first as an interest in the appropriate use of land. It came first from the notion of land planning. It affected the size of a site that you negotiated with a government for a school or a housing estate. It affected the way people live. The ability to move out of buildings and the ability to move in a pleasant environment was seen very early on as a necessity in our housing estates. I used to fight quite hard to make sure that we had enough land so that a housing estate would have enough land for people to be able to go out and get together. Then there was the question of taking that land and adapting it to the use of sick people who were ambulant for the first time and needed to be able to walk around in an appropriate space, or children who were playing outdoors and not just locked into buildings. The notion of upgrading that sort of space was very much a result of the language of the architecture of the world we are living in. You cannot go to a place like the Taj Mahal without being acutely aware of the site use and that is true of most of these great historic buildings. The use of gardens and water is a very strong part of Islam, in its references in the theological context to the quality of the environment. This is true in literature, poetry and art as well. That, in a sense, was a part of the inheritance, it was not anything particularly new. The thing that was new was the question: "Where do we have that talent?" We did not have it. Architectural offices were not particularly well-equipped for landscape design in the 1950s or 1960s.

PJ: It seems that there was a transition in the nature of the projects you were undertaking when you created the Aga Khan University in Karachi, beginning in the early 1970s.

His Highness the Aga Khan: Building the University was really a part of a process. It started with requests from leaders of civil society in the government of Pakistan, or from provincial governments in the country. They were acutely aware of the insufficient availability of doctors and the insufficiency of the quality of education. That na-

The Aga Khan and his brother, Prince Amyn, visiting the Northern Areas of Pakistan in 1996.

tional need was also reflected in the Ismaili community. I made an offer to the city authorities to build a medical school in Karachi. We had hospitals elsewhere so it was not outside our domain of work. The more we developed the project, the more it became clear that the notion of a medical school in a country like Pakistan was not viable. This was because a medical school not affiliated with a university did not have degree-giving powers. In order to give medical or nursing degrees, the school would have had to have been linked to an existing university. We determined that we had to negotiate to obtain the right for this medical school to be a university in its own right, an independent degree-giving institution. That was something I had not envisaged when I talked about building a medical school. The first step was to see if this idea was realistic. At the time, Muhammad Zia-ul-Haq was in power. He was acutely aware of the medical problems of his country because he had a daughter who had limitations. I went to see him and I thought it was going to be an extremely complex discussion. Here was somebody going to the President of the country saying: "For the first time in the history of your country will you agree that a self-governing private university should come into existence?" I thought that he would have to face a completely negative response from the public universities, and that he would therefore find it quite difficult to move forward on this idea. However, when he became President, he kept one ministry under his direct control, and that was the Ministry of Health. He was President and Minister of Health at the time that I spoke to him. I expected the discussion to last well over an hour and I obviously had a number of arguments to put forward. After the first sentence and a half, he cut me off, and he said: "Yes." It was an absolutely remarkable situation. At that stage, the whole process started going the other way. We were no longer talking about a medical school, we were talking about a university. The question became: "What should be the nature of a new self-governing university, with no academic limitations, coming into Pakistan and functioning within the context of the Ismaili Imamat?" That is when Derek Bok and Harvard became involved. The actual programme of the medical school was now seen as part of a wider scheme of things and it was not just about medicine in Pakistan. It was a host of other subjects, in Pakistan, in the *umma*[2] and even outside the *umma*, in the developing world.

If you are going to build a new university campus, within what context do you build it in Pakistan? That is when we initiated an extensive search for architects. We did not find any architects qualified in university design who had ever undertaken such a task in the Islamic world. We were looking for the unfindable, and we ran a competition. Tom Payette and his team were willing to learn. They carried out a number of journeys at our request to go and see the pluralism of architecture in the Islamic world, to try to synthesize some of the lessons that it taught us, and to bring some of these ideas of the quality of life that come out of Islamic society into the design of the university. We were looking at the quality of life. We were looking at the way in which Islamic architecture uses open spaces, the way temperature or heat is managed. We were also looking at the way users congregate or do not congregate, the way women will be with women and men with men. All of these things became the driving concepts. We were concerned with getting the concepts identified before designing the buildings, and that is what has caused the complex that you see there today.

PJ: Many of the buildings Tom Payette went to see were religious ones. Do you see a religious significance in architecture even where a religious function is not part of the programme, in the Aga Khan University for example?

His Highness the Aga Khan: In much of Islamic architecture you find a sense of spirituality. You find that spirituality not only in religious buildings. If you think of the history of landscape architecture and you relate that to references to heaven in the Koran, you find very strong statements about the value of the environment, the response to the senses, to scent, to noise, music or water. I think that in a number of spaces in the Islamic world, which are not religious buildings, there is a heightened sense of spirituality. You do not treat these spaces as theological spaces, you treat them as spaces that aim to give you a sense of spiritual happiness, of spiritual enjoyment. In a funny way, Azhar Park has some of that. We have carried out surveys on visitor reactions and a large percentage of visitors to this park in Cairo talk about spirituality. These are everyday visitors.

PJ: Might this be a spirituality that is not related only to Islam?

His Highness the Aga Khan: Yes. It is in a much wider sense. Many faiths have such forces that manifest themselves. You can enter a non-Muslim space that has a strong spiritual meaning and you will recognize it.

PJ: Many of the projects selected for the Aga Khan Award for Architecture have put an emphasis on the well-being of people. Is the Award not more about the well-being of people than it is about architecture in the sense usually used by the professional community, particularly in the West?

His Highness the Aga Khan: Yes, I think that is correct. The Award was born out of concern for the quality of life, rather than just the professional dynamics of architecture as it has been known in the Western world. In fact, we saw that as a moral obligation. Had we restricted this notion only to parts of the developing world which were "architectured", we would have been dealing with five per cent of the buildings. The vast majority of buildings in the developing world are not "architectured" buildings in the sense of the Western profession. That does not mean that quality buildings do not happen. They happen through a whole series of different processes, and not just the architectural process. The inherited knowledge of builders is remarkable. There is a whole body of inherited knowledge in developing countries, and in the Islamic world in particular, which is not driven by Western definitions of architecture. When the Award started, the question arose about whether we were talking about that small window of "architectured" buildings in this enormous environment or whether we were talking about the whole process of change of that environment? This was an issue that was debated extensively by people involved with the Award, in the Steering Committee in particular. Very early on there was consensus that the Aga Khan Award could not be just for "architectured" buildings, it had to be an award for quality buildings no matter what the process of their creation. We were looking at bringing those processes on board and enhancing them, rather than saying there is a divide between the professionally trained architect and the builder who comes out of a traditional society, who is a fantastic artist, but who may not have all the technical niceties of the modern architect. The Award was very definitely an initiative to recognize the processes of building quality.

PJ: The situation has changed a great deal since you created the Award in the late 1970s. Do you feel a need for the Award to evolve?

His Highness the Aga Khan: I think that the Award must evolve. Institutions that do not evolve tend to get marginalized. There are needs ahead of us which must be addressed by the Award. The biggest concern I would have is to recognize the processes of change, and to be certain that the Award plays an appropriate role in working with those processes so that they are not exclusive of quality in design or environmental concerns. There is a massive change in what I would call the symbols of high profile. In the 1950s and 1960s, the government was almost the only major client in these countries for high-profile buildings. That has changed enormously. There are private-sector buildings or mixed-use structures, but high-profile architecture is no longer reserved to governments. Secondly, there have been massive changes in the economies. Economies are being liberalized and housing estates are driven by property developers more than by government ministries. Even hospitals and schools are no longer driven by governments, but by others. Cities have become totally different from what they were fifty years ago. The process of urbanization is having an impact. I think what we should be talking about is the absolute need to improve the quality of life in rural environments. In the Western world, people tend to forget that seventy to eighty per cent of the populations of these countries live in rural environments. Of course the process of urbanization is taking place, but to go from seventy per cent to the situation in the United States where perhaps two to three per cent of the population is really rural, that swing is decades ahead in the developing world, and hopefully it will never happen. If it did, cities would be unliveable. As we enhance the productivity of agriculture, small commerce and leisure activities, we have to bring a better quality of life to the rural environments. The Award has already asked for nominators to give us the good village school or medical centre.

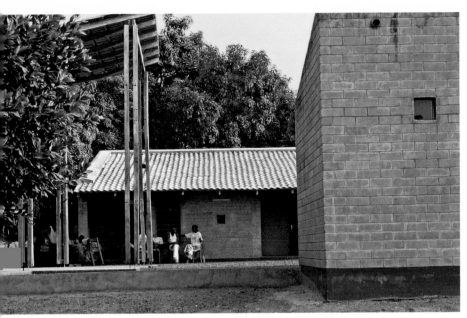

The Kahere Eila Poultry Farming School, Koliagbe, Guinea. Architects: Heikkinen-Komonen, winner of a 2001 Aga Khan Award for Architecture. "A fine example of an elegantly humble yet modern architecture," according to the 2001 Master Jury.

Whatever we can do to improve the quality of life in the rural environment is critical.

PJ: I understood that one of the reasons you created the Award was because the modern architecture in certain areas was getting out of hand, perhaps giving far more importance to superficial style than to substance and quality. Has not a new variant of that trend come back today in an even stronger way in some cities in the Persian Gulf for example?

His Highness the Aga Khan: One of the factors leading to the Award was what I would call the deconstruction of the cultural inheritance. This was part of the initial discussions of the Award. We were worried about the loss of cultural continuity in the physical environment. Problems came from a number of areas such as education. There was no serious analysis of traditions and how they came into place, or how they could be revived and used in modern buildings. That involved us in restoration as well, because we needed to learn about these great buildings. The pedagogical aspects and the idea of continuity were very important for the Award. The issue of modernity, which is the one you are addressing, was an extremely complex issue for us, and remains so. What we are talking about is forces in building that did not really exist at the time when the great buildings of the past were built. Airports, business complexes, housing estates, industries, office buildings, many phenomena of modern life clearly do not have a link with the past. How do you deal with that? You are stuck because you want these buildings to reflect the highest level of programmatic competence. I would be very unhappy if somebody were to put USD 50 million into a modern hospital without worrying about the quality of the medical care it was going to give. First and foremost an

airport has to be functional. It can have a lovely design, but if it is dysfunctional, you are in trouble. We ran into the problem of wanting to underwrite the full acceptance of the modern programme and the modern building. But then the question arises of how you make that culturally appropriate, or do you ignore that issue completely? That is what we are dealing with all the time in the Award today. We do not want to be seen as an institution that draws its inspiration only from the past. The inspiration is part of society, it is part of design. Our interest is to generate new inspirations for modern architecture, and I think that that is happening. One of the basic questions we have asked for which no Jury has given an answer is: "Is there one building which is so exceptional from a global point of view that the Award might select just that one building?" That question has been on the table since the Award was founded, and the answer has been: "No." This is, in a sense, evidence that the processes of change are underway, but they have not created, in the view of the Juries, that exceptional building which is of global meaning. It is true that the Gulf has taken in a number of the forces that play on Western societies, economics in particular.

PJ: You have just completed a new Ismaili Centre and Jamatkhana in Dubai that calls on Fatimid tradition in the design conceived by Rami El Dahan and Soheir Farid. In a way this building is at the opposite end of the scale from the towers presently rising in Dubai. Is it a deliberate gesture on your part to point out that there is another direction for architecture, or is that not the message?

His Highness the Aga Khan: The great expansion in construction there has to do with buildings that do not have a religious function. Economics are causing this to happen. I certainly did not want to create anything other than a human-scale building. The Award has sometimes discussed the question of scale. The whole debate about the tallest building in the world concerns ambition, vanity, pride, or whatever you want to call it. These are not particularly strong forces in our value system. I wanted a building there that was historically correct, and, secondly, I wanted it to be on a human scale.

PJ: Although not for a religious building, you are calling on the Japanese architect Fumihiko Maki to create two very contemporary structures in Canada, the Delegation of the Ismaili Imamat in Ottawa and the Aga Khan Museum in Toronto. Might Dubai not have been a place for an extremely modern design?

His Highness the Aga Khan: Absolutely. The fact is, however, that in the Middle East we are in a region that better justified such contexualization. In Canada the question was what issues the members of the community felt should be addressed. There was a sense that they wanted to be seen as forward-looking, educated people who could remain true to their traditions but were not fearful of modernity or the future. They wanted in a sense to Islamicize modernity rather than to have modernity impact Islam. We did a survey to try to understand what the younger generations in Canada were thinking. If we were going to build a building that was going to be there for fifty years or whatever, what should that building be? They were talking about aspirations for the future; they were talking about integrating themselves with the environment in which they live, which is an environment of quality modern buildings. They were looking for modernity, but they were also looking for empathy with Islamic traditions. We have that empathy. We have not gone to an anti-cultural building, but rather a cultural building where the inspiration is modernity plus some of the value systems from the Islamic world. One of them is open space.

PJ: You also wrote to Professor Maki, in the context of the Delegation of the Ismaili Imamat building in Ottawa, about the value of light.

His Highness the Aga Khan: One of the issues in the Islamic world is the relationship between an ability to create and what we see of that creation. Nature is one of the evidences for a Muslim of God's creation. I am personally very sensitive to that. That is why, for example, in the Delegation building I gave Professor Maki the idea of rock crystal. Rock crystal is an extraordinary natural phenomenon. It plays with light, and in our world that is very important; it has a quasi-mystical component because, depending on the angle under which it is viewed, you see it differently. It has many facets both literally and figuratively that are fascinating.

PJ: With Fumihiko Maki are you not calling on a different type of architect than the ones you have worked with in the past? Is he not more of an international 'star' than some others you have called on? For the University of Central Asia you have selected another well-known Japanese figure, the architect Arata Isozaki.

His Highness the Aga Khan: If the mandate to the architect is to be as good as any in modern architecture, using modern materials and concepts but at the same time having the sensitivity to bring in external value systems, Maki was the obvious choice, because of the sensitivity of Japanese architects to their own cultural history. Linking cultural history to modernity is probably something that Japanese architects are as good at as anyone. They understand that. Maki seemed to be one to whom you could give a mandate and say, I am trying to bridge a number of different forces by building this modern building, and one of them is to take some of the value systems of the past, put them into this building, but not make it so esoteric that it overburdens you. It has to be inspirational and subtle. It is not a theological building, but if, within that building, there are spaces of spirituality, which we like to see as part of everyday life – it is not the exception, it should be part of everyday life –, then you are bringing that into that building. His concept of the *chahar-bagh* and the roof of the Delegation building which plays with light and facets of glass, to me is very inspirational. I am the client. Most of the people working in that building will be working for what I would call human purposes. They are not working for capitalist purposes. They will be there to serve people, and that is a different exercise. Even the staff of the Aga Khan Fund for Economic Development (AKFED) in that building will be trying to build economic change in societies that need it. The

The Aga Khan photographed in November 2005 during a site visit to Bagh-i Babur (the Babur Gardens) in Kabul, Afghanistan. The group is in the Queen's Palace; to the right of the Aga Khan looking at a plan of restoration work in progress is Prince Amyn, behind him, Abdullah Abdullah, the Foreign Minister of Afghanistan.

Right, ablution fountain (*sabil*), 13th century AD, in the central courtyard of the Ahmad Ibn Tulun Mosque (AD 876–879), Cairo, Egypt.

Aga Khan Fund for Economic Development is not a holding company, it is a development company. It takes risks, some of them very severe, and very few venture capital companies are still doing that today. We believe that there is a whole category of least-developed countries which are greatly in need of economic change. Therefore, the venture capital company of the past still needs to exist.

With Mr Isozaki the mandate is much less driven by architectural inheritance than it would have been in other places. The reason for that is the wish of local governments. The wish of the local governments, and I should think of society generally, has been to disconnect from the past. They are looking for the "disconnect" that is inspirational for their future, drawn from creation as it is today in the architectural context, rather than the inherited past, because the inherited past represents a large number of symbols that they do not like. The point with Isozaki was to come up with something that is specific to the future without a connection to the past. It has to be specific and desirable in three different countries (Kazakhstan, Kyrgyzstan and Tajikistan). What we are

trying to do is to create spaces and places that are disconnected from the past, but bring a value system for the future. What are those value systems?

PJ: Is it fair to state that building has become one of the most significant parts of your action as Imam?

His Highness the Aga Khan: That is for others to say. This part of my work enters and exits my daily existence according to what needs to be done. It is part of the mandate of the Imam to improve the quality of life of members of the community. As I told you at the beginning of our discussion, that fact causes you to look at the physical environment. You cannot conceive of quality-of-life change without integrating the physical environment. Everyday you live under a roof.

PJ: Building is, in a sense, a way of bringing people together.

His Highness the Aga Khan: Yes, or of giving them a sense of individuality. Sometimes they also need that. I think spirituality is not necessarily experienced only in a societal context, it can be very much an individual thing. There are certain times when you need to create space where spirituality can be experienced individually. I think of parks as places where the individual is very powerful. We have also worked recently on dormitories for universities. What the West would think of as secular spaces, in our context are very often not exclusively secular. They actually seek to contain, in an area or in the totality of the building, a space which has an additional message or an additional sense to it. If you walk through the Aga Khan University in Karachi, there are a number of spaces on that campus that are very unique I think. In the Islamic world we always look at the relation between *din*[3] and *dunya*[4] and we cannot tolerate that one functions without the other. The notion of *din* and *dunya* and the integrity of human life is a very important issue.

---

1 The Karakoram is a mountain range spanning the borders between Pakistan, China and India, located in the regions of Gilgit, Ladakh and Baltistan.
2 The all-embracing Islamic community.
3 Usually translated as "religion".
4 Usually translated as "this world".

THE AGA KHAN AWARD FOR ARCHITECTURE: 1977–2007 AND BEYOND

The Aga Khan Award for Architecture: 1977–2007 and Beyond

The Aga Khan Award for Architecture, established in 1977 by His Highness the Aga Khan, "recognizes examples of architectural excellence that encompass contemporary design, social housing, community improvement and development, restoration, reuse and area conservation, as well as landscaping and environmental issues." Organized on the basis of three-year cycles, the Award is governed by a Steering Committee chaired by the Aga Khan. The Steering Committee in turn selects a Master Jury that chooses the Award winners from a series of several hundred nominations that come from a broad network of architects and other interested parties. Both the Steering Committee and the Master Jury have been marked by the presence of such internationally recognized architects as Hassan Fathy, Charles Correa, Frank Gehry, Zaha Hadid, Fumihiko Maki, Jacques Herzog, Glenn Murcutt, Ricardo Legoretta and Farshid Moussavi. More unusual, however, has been the continued and significant presence of philosophers, sociologists, academics or artists, whether from the Muslim world or not. The Award "seeks to identify and encourage building concepts that successfully address the needs and aspirations of societies in which Muslims have a significant presence."[1] The Aga Khan Award for Architecture differs from other prizes in many respects, one being that buildings must be visited by experts before being considered by the Jury. Other innovative aspects are the association of clients with the architects for each prize, but also the willingness to "premiate" buildings or schemes that help people even if they are far from the mainstream of architectural criticism and thought. The Award has completed nine cycles of activity since 1977, and documentation has been compiled on over 7500 building projects located throughout the world.

The Aga Khan Award has often been compared to other prizes, such as the Pritzker, given to a single already famous architect each year, and yet its purpose and scope are very different. Robert Campbell of *The Boston Globe* called it the "wisest prize programme in architecture." And Martin Filler wrote in *The New Republic* that the award "has had a demonstrable effect in improving the quality of Islamic architecture during the same period that the Pritzker has merely stoked the global celebrity machine."[2] Writing in *The New Republic* in 2005, Clay Risen said: "Indeed, more than fifty years since its publication, it is Ayn Rand's *The Fountainhead* and its architect-hero, Howard Roark … who provide the model for architectural appreciation. After Roark (and his real-life inspiration, Frank Lloyd Wright), we see buildings primarily as useful works of art, the imposition of the artist-architect's will on society and the human landscape. Contrast this with the Aga Khan awards, which look at architecture as an element of culture, and culture as an element of material progress; as something worthwhile in itself, but ultimately worthy because it is a means to something else. Obviously such a view would limit an appreciation for individual genius, because no matter how witty or beautiful a building, its value – to society, to the Aga Khan awards – is measured in how well it serves its community."[3] The opinions of American journalists are of course tangential insofar as the nature of the Award is concerned. Their reactions do make clear, however, that the Award has set out on a different path than other architecture prizes, seeking to give precedence to buildings and other realizations that help people and give constructive examples to architects and clients. In this, it actually challenges the existing international architectural 'system' far more than might at first be apparent.

What has the Aga Khan Award for Architecture really accomplished and what are its goals for the future? No more informed opinion on the subject exists than that of the Aga Khan himself. In response to the question of why he established this institution in the first place, he states: "It is now twenty-seven years since the Award was launched. At that time, I was becoming increasingly disturbed by the loss of cultural identity and appropriateness in the architecture and built environments of much of the Muslim world. A few centuries ago, architecture was one of the great forms of artistic expression in the many diverse Muslim societies … But in recent years, Islamic architecture seemed to have lost its identity – I should perhaps say identities – and its inspiration. Occasionally, construction tended to repeat previous Islamic styles, but much more often, it simply absorbed imported architectural forms, language and materials."[4] What has the Award accomplished? "We broadened the definition of architecture from one that tended to look only at individual structures to one that encompassed entire neighbourhoods, including informal settlements, village communities and open public spaces. In the first nine cycles, some 2661 projects have been assessed and documented in eighty-eight countries, an unparalleled data resource base. The independent Master Juries have recognized ninety-seven projects in twenty-five countries."[5]

Despite the scale and demonstrable importance of the Award, the Aga Khan remains committed to going further still. "We have much yet to strive for," he declared in New Delhi. "But I believe the process we have launched has become a self-sustaining and unstoppable force for change in the human habitat not only in the Muslim world, but in much of the developing world as well. The larger and perhaps more interesting question is whether this approach might be adopted to support other cultures that are at risk. The issues we have been attempting to address through the process of the Aga Khan Award for Architecture are not exclusive to the Muslim world. The non-Muslim world struggles equally with explosive population growth, poverty, environmental degradation, exodus from rural areas, globalization and the impact on cultural identity of new forms of media … Perhaps these lessons will one day be seen as an important contribution from the Muslim world: a contribution to the broader cause of maintaining and enhancing a multicultural, pluralist world and a responsive, appropriate human habitat."[6]

1 See: http://www.akdn.org/agency/aktc_akaa.html#intro.
2 Martin Filler, 'Eyes on the Prize', in: The New Republic, 3 May 1999.
3 Clay Risen, 'The Pritzker v. The Aga Khan. Prize Fight', in: The New Republic Online, 16 February 2005.
4 Address by His Highness the Aga Khan at the Ninth Award Cycle of the Aga Khan Award for Architecture, New Delhi, 27 November 2004.
5 Ibid.
6 Ibid.

Water Towers

KUWAIT CITY, KUWAIT

Architect: Vatten – Byggnadsbyzan (VBB)/
                     Lindström & Björn Design
Client: Ministry of Electricity and Water,
                     Kuwait City, Kuwait
Completed: 1976
                     AKAA 1980 Cycle

■ The First Cycle of the Aga Khan Award for Architecture (1978–80) selected a total of fifteen projects in specific categories such as the 'Search for Consistency with Historical Context' or 'Social Premises for Future Architectural Development'. The Jury, which included the noted architects Kenzo Tange (1913–2005) and Giancarlo de Carlo (1919–2005), wrote in its report: "We found our task a difficult one. The difficulty arose from the prevailing reality that Muslim culture is slowly emerging from a long period of subjugation and neglect in which it had virtually lost its identity, its self-confidence, its very language – those characteristics which, after all, are what relevant architecture does and should express. The present is a period of transition – a period when traditional heritage is being rediscovered, when new experiments are being made to combine modern technology with cultural continuity in both richer and poorer countries, and when there is urgent search for socially responsive forms of architecture for the poor majority." It may be that the most visually arresting of the awards was given in the category 'Search for Innovation' to a series of Water Towers completed in Kuwait City in 1976. Part of the programme launched by the Ministry of Electricity and Water to build a total of thirty-three such towers, the most prominent site is situated in the northern part of the city, on the Cape of Ras-Ajuza which projects into the waters of the Persian Gulf. At the time of their completion, but also at other critical moments such as the First Gulf War (1990–91) when they suffered shell and bullet damage, the image of the Kuwait Towers came to symbolize the entire region. The main tower of this group consists in a hollow concrete column 187 metres high supporting two spheres. The larger sphere contains a restaurant, banquet hall, indoor garden and cafeteria. The lower half of the sphere is a reservoir with a capacity of 4500 cubic metres. The smaller sphere above it is 123-metres high and houses a café and a revolving observatory that completes a full turn every thirty minutes. The second tower of the group, not accessible to the public, supports a spherical water tank. The spheres of both towers are "surfaced in steel plates enamelled in bright colours, serving as sun reflectors and inspired by mosaic-surfaced Islamic domes." A concrete needle containing electrical equipment is equipped with floodlights that illuminate the other two towers, creating one of the most emblematic contemporary architectural compositions in the Middle East. The towers were commended by the Jury "for a bold attempt to integrate modern technology, aesthetic values, functional needs and social facilities in a public facility." Designed by the Swedes Sune Lindström and Malene Björn, and built between 1971 and 1976 by a Serbian company, the Kuwait Towers opened to the public in March 1979. They are seen locally as a symbol of "development and continued progress" though their genesis and realization was largely in the hands of Europeans. As the Master Jury commented on the whole of their selections: "In most instances they represented not the ultimate in architectural excellence, but steps in a process of discovery, still an incomplete voyage toward many promising frontiers."

The most prominently sited of the thirty-three water towers built by the Ministry of Electricity and Water in the 1970s are these, located in Kuwait City on the Cape of Ras-Ajuza on the Persian Gulf.

Agricultural Training Centre

NIANING, SENEGAL

Architect: UNESCO/BREDA (Kamal El Jack,
Pierre Bussat, Oswald Dellicour, Sjoerd
Nienhuys, Christophorus Posma and
Paul de Wallik), Dakar, Senegal

Master Mason: D'Iallo, Dakar, Senegal

Client: Ministry of Education, Dakar, Senegal

Sponsor: CARITAS (Frère Romuald Picard), Dakar,
Senegal

Completed: 1977

          AKAA 1980 Cycle

The high, arching interior space seen in the image to the left may recall architecture of the past, but it is both original and adapted to the circumstances. It is neither a pastiche nor an attempt to imitate Western models.

■ In a sense, this project might be seen as the diametrical opposite of the Kuwait Towers. Selected in the category 'Search for Innovation', it was made with load-bearing sand and cement walls, with masonry arches supporting barrel vaults. As the documentation of the Aga Khan Award describes it: "The vaults, whose thickness at the crown is only a little over four centimetres, were formed using three layers of cement mortar stabilized with wire mesh at the top of the vault. Rounded plywood struts were used to support the shuttering formed from millet matting. Buttresses counteract the horizontal thrust of the vaults."[1] The Jury praised the project as displaying "a complete architectural language whose forms, sober and beautiful at the same time, correspond to its social ambience. A labour-intensive building system has been used here to revitalize masonry construction by training a local craftsman who in turn has trained others. It has thus provided a model for a number of different projects in Senegal." The elegance and simplicity of the Agricultural Training Centre might never have attracted international attention without the existence of the Aga Khan Award for Architecture, and this in itself is a considerable realization. It might be said that in the selection of this type of project, the Aga Khan Award first set itself apart from other architecture prizes the world over. The structural innovation implied is naturally more of importance on a local scale than it is vis-à-vis developed countries. While architecture prizes and professional publications have always tended to put forward cutting-edge technology and design, here it is the local use of a combination of time-honoured techniques that drew the Ju-

ry's attention. It happens that the Agricultural Training Centre in Nianing is located in a country that is ninety-four per cent Muslim, but the solutions employed, based on a UNESCO prototype, are suited to other developing countries, of whatever religion. This lesson is still valid today, even though the Aga Khan Award was given to this project in 1980. Although the significance of the Aga Khan Award does not lie in any particular project, but rather in a method and a list of selected projects, the Jury's recognition in this instance of the kind of architecture that can actually help people who need assistance bears witness to a ground-breaking approach. What if architecture were not only about astonishing new forms and ever larger modern buildings, but rather about the people who use it? What if an award sought out the kind of architecture that improves the lot of the world's poor, or disfavoured, be they Muslim or of other religions? The generosity of the patron of the Award bears fruit with this selection. Making this local success known on an international scale can only have positive implications.

1 See: http://www.akdn.org/agency/akaa/firstcycle/agricultural.html.

Images of the
Training Centre in
use emphasize the
insistence of the
Aga Khan Award
for Architecture on
seeing and evaluating
completed projects,
a process that
differentiates the
Award from most
comparable prizes.

Hajj Terminal, King Abdul Aziz International Airport

JEDDAH, SAUDI ARABIA

Architect:	Skidmore, Owings & Merrill (Fazlur Rahman Khan, Engineer), New York and Chicago
Client:	Ministry of Defence and Aviation, Riyadh, Saudi Arabia
Completed:	1981–82
	AKAA 1983 Cycle

And proclaim the Pilgrimage among men. They will come to thee on foot and (mounted) on every kind of camel, lean on account of journeys through deep and distant mountain highways …

Koran 22:27

■ The Hajj, the pilgrimage to Mecca, is the fifth of the Five Pillars of Islam and every able-bodied Muslim is required to make this pilgrimage at least once in their lifetime. Although the tradition of the Hajj dates from the year AD 632, as recently as 1950 the number of pilgrims was under 100,000 per year. The total exceeded one million for the first time in 1983, just after the completion of the new Terminal, with the vast majority arriving by air. Statistics from the Saudi Ministry of Hajj show that more than two million people fulfilled this obligation in 2006. The airport in Jeddah, near Mecca, is thus called on to handle an exceptional influx of visitors in short periods of time, an unusual requirement for a modern airport. The Hajj Terminal, designed by the American architects Skidmore, Owings & Merrill, can receive approximately 50,000 people for up to eighteen hours in the arrival period and as many as 80,000 for up to thirty-six hours during departure. The description of the building in the documents of the Aga Khan Award is instructive: "Roofed by a fabric tension structure that covers more area (40.5 hectares) than any roof in the world, the terminal provides toilets, shops, benches and banking facilities for the pilgrims. Twenty-one tent units, each forty-five metres square, form a single module. The terminal is comprised of ten such modules: two identical five-module sections separated by a landscaped mall. Thus, the two large terminal units each comprise a total of 105 tents. The tents are hooked to steel rings hung from suspension cables that are draped from single pylons in the interior of the module, from ladder-like double pylons at the module edges and from four-pylon towers at the corners. The enclosed and air-conditioned arrival buildings are located under the tents along the outside edge of the terminal units parallel to the aircraft aprons."[1] As this description suggests, this is a technologically correct solution to the problem posed by modern vernacular architecture. Though the architects may come from Chicago or New York, they have proposed a solution that is appropriate and indeed innovative.

In the Second Cycle of the Aga Khan Award (1981–83), the Master Jury, including Ismaïl Serageldin, Charles Moore, Roland Simounet and James Stirling, selected eleven projects from a total of 216 nominated for their review. The Jury Report stated emphatically: "The Hajj Terminal, almost everyone felt, is in a class by itself, its structure a magnificent achievement of twentieth-century technology."[2] Although it does not have the prominent profile and urban location that made the Kuwait Towers so symbolic, the Hajj Terminal clearly demonstrates that modern technology and, indeed, the intervention of Western architects can be put to fruitful use in the modernization of facilities specifically intended for use in the Muslim world. In this instance, the symbolism is visible to all those who pass through the Hajj Terminal.

1 See: http://www.akdn.org/agency/akaa/secondcycle/saudiarabia.html.
2 See: http://www.akdn.org/agency/akaa/secondcycle/mj_83.htm.

Intended for vast numbers of pilgrims, the Hajj Terminal
employs a vocabulary inspired by tents, but renders it
both contemporary and appropriate to the circumstances.
The very lightness of the architecture sets it apart in the
world of airport terminals.

Great Mosque

NIONO, MALI

Designer/Master Mason: Lassina Minta, Niono, Mali
Client: Muslim Community of Niono, Mali
Completed: 1973
  AKAA 1983 Cycle

■ Despite its rather ancient appearance, this mosque was originally built in the centre of the village of Niono, near the south-western edge of the Upper Niger Delta between 1945 and 1948. Too small for the needs of the local Muslim community, the mosque was successively enlarged to reach an area of 726 square metres. Built by a local mason with the assistance of members of the congregation and financed by the community, the mosque is based on traditional forms found in Djenné or Mopti. Load-bearing walls and pillars of sun-dried clay bricks are topped by a roof made of local wood. Imported wood and corrugated iron were used, as was precast concrete for the window frames and tubular steel posts for the veranda. In this sense, although the structure was created almost exclusively with traditional methods and materials, it does not hesitate to call on some modern supplies where they were required. Unlike painstaking restorations that would have eschewed corrugated iron for example, the local people in charge of the project took a much more natural, progressive approach to their design and construction. The Aga Khan Award description of the project points out that "the construction techniques and materials, load-bearing mud-brick walls and arches supporting floors and roofs of wood, matting and earth have been used in the region for centuries. The structural module is determined by the length of wood available. Each mud-brick pier supports the springing of arches in four directions. The arches in turn support the flat span of the roof."[1] Few other architecture awards could have reunited such diverse projects as the Hajj Terminal in Jeddah and this mosque. In a sense, this diversity, confirmed from cycle to cycle, is the reflection not only of the nature of the process and goals laid out by His Highness the Aga Khan, but also of the very diversity and varying needs of Muslims in very different parts of the world. That outsiders, many of them Westerners, should notice and then single out what is a valid solution for contemporary needs through the use of traditional forms and methods is an unexpected form of encouragement, far from the winds of fashion that blow across the more 'sophisticated' world of contemporary architecture. The selection of the Niono Mosque for an Aga Khan Award represents a sensitive call to appreciate the values and adaptive capacities of the past. The fact that the project emerged from the work and needs of the people of the village makes it all the more a valid example. The 1983 Master Jury stated: "The continuing existence of traditional forms – both sophisticated and primitive – is one of our strongest allies in retaining architectural character and cultural identity as large-scale modern industry and worldwide building models assert their presence. Hence the will and the conscious intention to continue the tradition should be commended and encouraged."

1 See: http://www.akdn.org/agency/akaa/secondcycle/mali.html.

Similar in form to other Malian mosques such as those in Djenné or Mopti, the Great Mosque in Niono includes a number of windows for ventilation. It is located in the centre of the town, near the market. The mosque is financed and maintained by the local community.

National Assembly Building

S H E R - E - B A N G L A   N A G A R ,   D H A K A ,
B A N G L A D E S H

Architect:	Louis I. Kahn, Philadelphia, with David Wisdom and Associates (after 1979), Philadelphia
Client:	Public Works Department, Dhaka, Bangladesh
Completed:	1983
	AKAA 1989 Cycle

■ The Master Jury for the Fourth Cycle of the Aga Khan Award (1987–89) included architects Geoffrey Bawa (Sri Lanka), Charles Correa (India) and Kamran Diba (Iran), as well as Professors William Porter and Oleg Grabar from MIT and Harvard who had been instrumental in the creation of the Award. They selected eleven projects, a number of which might be considered unusual or prescient in terms of the reasoning behind the votes. Amongst these, the National Assembly Building in Dhaka, Bangladesh, by Louis I. Kahn (1902–74) was a famous building before it was completed, in part because of the identity of the architect, but also because of its association with the emerging identity of a nation. It was in 1959 that the government of Pakistan decided to create a 'second capital' in East Pakistan with an Assembly Building to be located in Dhaka. Louis Kahn was called on to design the building in 1962 and work began in 1966, only to be interrupted by the civil war that eventually gave birth to Bangladesh in 1971. As Darab Diba wrote in his 1989 Technical Review for the Award, the Dhaka building was influenced "by classical antiquity (Roman baths, pantheons, and so on) and the overall process of the Beaux-Arts education of the past two centuries, as well as Islamic, pre-Mughal and Mughal architecture (Mughal mausoleum of Humayun in Delhi, the Red Fort at Agra, Lalbagh Fort, Bharatpur, Bagh-e Mosque, and so on)." It was thus never intended to be a specifically Muslim building, but rather "endeavours to be a universal symbol of intelligence and the order of social structures." The heart of the complex is the assembly chamber, a thirty-metre-high domed amphitheatre with 300 seats. Eight "light and air courts" and a restaurant are part of the design, which is marked by its deeply

set windows intended to provide shelter from wind and rain and the use of rough shuttered fair-faced concrete inlaid with bands of white marble. It has been described as a kind of hollow concrete column with perforated walls. Diba underlines that the existence of the building played an important role in the emergence of the country's first school of architecture (inaugurated in the 1960s) and that of the Institute of the Architects of Bangladesh (1972). Despite its notably eclectic sources of inspiration, Darab Diba noted that "the Assembly complex building has become the symbol of Bangladesh. It represents all the notions of order and social justice of a people living in need and poverty." He stated further: "Several leading architects have expressed the view that this building bears the essence and necessary link with the culture and architectural heritage of the country (for example, Mazhar ul-Islam, Bashirul Haq) and that the spatial and formal interpretation of this design actually reflects the general atmosphere of the country." Few buildings could have summed up the ambitions of the Aga Khan Award for Architecture as clearly as this one. This is because it seeks its sources in tradition, while remaining resolutely modern. It is integrated into a Muslim society in the most forward-looking way.

Louis Kahn's modernity is one that does not conflict with the past. His fortress-like massing in this instance surely evokes another era, but geometry, from plan to elevation, rules his architecture.

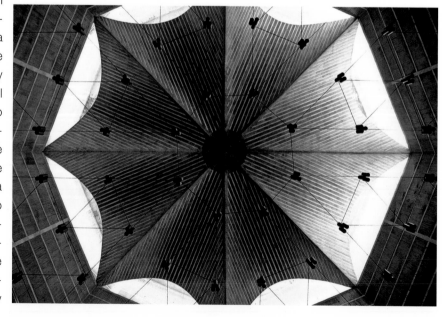

Institut du Monde Arabe

PARIS, FRANCE

Architect: Jean Nouvel, Pierre Soria and Gilbert
                  Lezénés with Architecture Studio, Paris
Consultant: Ziyad Ahmed Zaidan, Jeddah, Saudi
                  Arabia
Client: Institut du Monde Arabe, Paris, France
Completed: 1987
                  AKAA 1989 Cycle

■ The Institut du Monde Arabe was the first of François Mitterrand's 'Grand Travaux' projects. Its location, on the Left Bank of the Seine not far from Notre Dame Cathedral, destined the structure to be a landmark. Intended as a tribute to the Arab world, its art and culture, the Institute has 16,912 square metres of usable floor area and was built for a budget of 341 million francs (structure). Jean Nouvel emphasizes that the building is meant to be an intermediary between the Middle East and the West but also between the old and the new. Although it was one of the winners of the Aga Khan Award for Architecture in 1989, the Institute has relatively few actual references to Arab or Muslim design. In this respect however, its south facade, opposite the Seine, deserves mention. The architects used geometric motifs derived from Islamic decorative arts to create an entire wall inspired by the *mashrabiyya*. Its diaphragm-like openings were intended to open and close with varying light, but this system in fact never functioned properly. Despite this technical failure, the wall serves to bring ample but filtered light into the building and its exhibition areas. The filtering effect is indeed reminiscent of the use of light in Muslim architecture. Visitors questioned for the Aga Khan Award Technical Review by Attila Yücel in 1989 confirmed that they did not identify the building with Arab architecture, but some found this natural given that it is located in Paris. Set near the Jardin des Plantes and the Jussieu University campus, the IMA also marks the end of the Boulevard Saint Germain. Its long curved south wall sweeps along the quay with a studied modernity, at once integrated into the significant architecture in its environs and yet resolutely of its time. In this respect, despite the uncomfortable nature of many of its interior spaces, the building can be termed successful. It might

be noted in passing that many interior spaces designed by Jean Nouvel can be described as low and dark. The 1989 Master Jury agreed that the building is "at times overly complex to use with ease and comfort," but concluded that it can be seen as "a successful bridge between French and Arab cultures." This last remark may be the best response to those who questioned why a building built in Paris by French architects should even be considered for the Aga Khan Award. The response to this query lies not so much in the architecture as it does in the function of the building. Meant to be funded by twenty-two Arab countries, the Institute is a French foundation "conceived to make Arab culture known and to encourage cultural exchanges between France and the Arab world." In this sense, the building obviously qualifies for the Aga Khan Award.

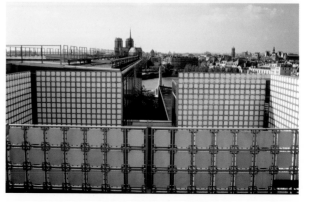

The Institut du Monde Arabe occupies a prominent Seine-side site in Paris, France, near the Austerlitz railway station and at the end of the Boulevard Saint-Germain.

Right, using the principle of the photographic diaphragm for the facade, the architects bring to mind the *mashrabiyya*.

The site of the building is close to that of Notre Dame Cathedral (right). Library or exhibition spaces are generous, contrasting with the more intimate or low-ceilinged entrance sequences. Meant to close according to light conditions, the window diaphragms do not function as planned.

The example given by micro-credit loans through the Grameen Bank in Bangladesh has inspired other programmes of the same nature throughout the world. In this instance, architecture, in the sense of the physical environment referred to by the Aga Khan, has been greatly improved for people in need.

Grameen Bank Housing Programme

VARIOUS LOCATIONS, BANGLADESH

Planner:	Grameen Bank (Muhammad Yunus, Director), Dhaka, Bangladesh
Client:	Landless Members of Grameen Bank, various locations, Bangladesh
Completed:	1984
	AKAA 1989 Cycle

We shall not live in dilapidated homes. We shall repair our homes and work toward constructing new houses at the earliest.

One of the "Sixteen Decisions" that borrowers undertake when they join the Grameen Bank Housing Programme

■ Despite the fact that the houses built in Bangladesh with Grameen Bank micro-credits might not have qualified for any other major architecture prize, the Master Jury of the Fourth Cycle of the Aga Khan Award recognized the efforts of Muhammad Yunus and his institution long before the Norwegian Nobel Committee. On 13 October 2006, the Committee announced that it had "decided to award the Nobel Peace Prize for 2006, divided into two equal parts, to Muhammad Yunus and Grameen Bank for their efforts to create economic and social development from below. Lasting peace cannot be achieved unless large population groups find ways in which to break out of poverty. Micro-credit is one such means. Development from below also serves to advance democracy and human rights."

In his 1989 Technical Review for the Aga Khan Award, John Norton wrote: "The Grameen Bank Housing Loan Programme has developed out of the Grameen Bank project which was started in 1976 to raise the incomes and the standard of living of the most disadvantaged sections of the rural community in Bangladesh through providing access to credit. The Housing Loans are an extension of the same policy and permit Grameen Bank members to borrow sums worth between USD 250 and USD 600 to build a new house ... The Grameen Bank requires that the roof be covered in corrugated iron sheeting supported by four reinforced-concrete columns manufactured by the bank. Housing loans began in 1984 and to date over 44,500 houses have been built by Grameen Bank members. The repayment rate, including 5% interest, is close to a hundred per cent." Together with the concrete columns, the Bank provides twenty-six corrugated-iron roofing sheets and a prefabricated sanitary slab.

According to the last issued annual report of the Grameen Bank (2004): "Ownership of a house infuses people with a sense of confidence, security and self-respect, to begin dreaming for a better life for herself and her family. A member can borrow up to BDT 25,000 for constructing a simple tin-roof house at an interest rate of 8% to be paid back over a period of ten years. Over 607,000 houses have been constructed with the housing loans averaging BDT 13,413 (Bangladesh Taka, equivalent in 2004 to USD 222). During 2004, 28,883 houses have been built with housing loans amounting to BDT 282.05 million (USD 4.75 million)." Whatever the interest and value of contemporary architecture, very few projects can claim to have improved the living conditions of so many extremely poor people. The Grameen Bank Housing Programme should obviously encourage some to re-evaluate their views of the importance of architecture and the nature of what constitutes a successful building. Acknowledging that the scope of such a project might well extend even beyond the Muslim world, the Master Jury stated that "the lesson of this success lies in the thoughtful concept and the participatory process behind it, which could be emulated, not imitated, throughout the Muslim and Third Worlds."

Kaedi Regional Hospital

KAEDI, MAURITANIA

Architect:	Association pour le Développement Naturel d'une Architecture et d'un Urbanisme Africains (ADAUA), Jak Vautherin (former Secretary General), Fabrizio Carol (Principal Architect), Birahim Niang (Assistant Architect) and Shamsuddin N'Dow (Engineer), Nouakchott, Mauritania
Client:	Ministry of Health, Nouakchott, Mauritania
Completed:	1989
	AKAA 1995 Cycle

■ The 1995 Master Jury, which included Peter Eisenman, Charles Jencks and Luis Monreal, selected twelve projects from 442 nominations and grouped them according to three themes: 'Projects that Address a Critical Social Discourse'; 'Projects that Address a Critical Architectural and Urbanistic Discourse'; and 'Projects that Introduce Innovative Concepts Worthy of Attention'. The Kaedi Regional Hospital in Mauritania was in the second of these categories. In the book published on the occasion of the 1995 Cycle, Cynthia Davidson wrote: "The Kaedi Hospital annex is an inventive project that enriches the vocabulary of brick-vaulted and domed building without using timber or reinforced concrete. After two years of experimentation with local materials and building forms and techniques, the architects created ribbed structures, pointed vaults and new shapes to match the needs of the various parts of the building ... The learned informality of the design is remarkable ... This is not a copy but an outstanding original, a lasting contribution to the art of building with brick structures."[1] Undertaken by ADAUA (Association for the Development of Traditional African Urbanism and Architecture), the Kaedi project clearly goes beyond traditional aid schemes. ADAUA is an organization established in 1975 in Ouagadougou, Burkina Faso, to "revive and promote indigenous African architecture and to train local inhabitants in appropriate technologies." Considering that Kaedi is located in a remote rural area of southern Mauritania on the Senegal River, the praise and the prestige associated with the Aga Khan Award for Architecture could never have come to such a project in other circumstances. The population of Mauritania is almost a hundred per cent Muslim, and, despite oil and iron ore deposits, the country qualified in 2000 for debt relief under the Heavily Indebted Poor Countries (HIPC) initiative and it is estimated that forty per cent of its population lives below the applicable poverty line. The extension of the Kaedi Hospital adds 120 beds to an existing hospital, including an operating theatre, paediatric, surgical and ophthalmic departments, a maternity and general medical unit, a laundry, kitchens, storerooms, a garage and a workshop. The Award documents for this project explain: "The architects were not to replicate the earlier hospital's conventional concrete-frame buildings; their brief was to house the planned facilities by developing new low-cost techniques of construction employing local materials and skills that would be applicable to other building types within the region. All workmen were local, trained on the site to perform the new techniques. Although the use of brick is not a part of the local vernacular, the architects chose to develop a structural vocabulary of handmade brick, fired in kilns built near the source of clay ... The Jury believes that the innovative construction techniques introduced may have wide significance, particularly since the successful functioning of the hospital should encourage similar initiatives elsewhere."[2]

1 Cynthia C. Davidson, 'Kaedi Regional Hospital', in: Cynthia C. Davidson and Ismaïl Serageldin (eds.), *Architecture Beyond Architecture*, London 1995.
2 See: http://www.akdn.org/agency/akaa/sixthcycle/mauritania.html.

Above left, self-supporting arches made with locally fired handmade bricks form the winding circulation corridors of the hospital.

Although the specific forms and materials of the hospital are not traditional ones in the region, the project actually developed what might be called a new archetype, employing a "learned informality" that could well be applied in other locations.

Mosque of the
Grand National Assembly

ANKARA, TURKEY

Architect:	Behruz and Can Cinici, Istanbul, Turkey
Client:	Turkish Grand National Assembly, Ankara, Turkey
Completed:	1989
	AKAA 1995 Cycle

■ A number of Aga Khan Awards for Architecture have gone to mosques, either for restoration, or, more rarely, for innovative, contemporary approaches. One intriguing case is that of the Mosque of the Grand National Assembly of Turkey. Composed of "a triangular forecourt and a rectangular prayer hall overlooking a large, triangular, terraced garden and pool," the structure lacks many traditional elements and might even be considered controversial because of its location. Writing in *Muqarnas*, a scientific journal published by the Aga Khan Program for Islamic Architecture (AKPIA) at Harvard, Mohammad Al-Asad wrote: "The mosque of the Turkish Grand National Assembly in Ankara designed by the Turkish father and son team of Behruz and Can Cinici represents a significant departure from the usual conception of mosque architecture, both past and present, in its clear rejection of elements that have traditionally been associated with the mosque: the traditional dome and minaret are absent; the traditionally solid *qibla* wall is in their design replaced by a glazed surface that opens onto a garden; and the separation between the men's and women's areas in its prayer hall is represented only by a set of steps that rise to about one metre. These di-

gressions from, or rejections of, past prototypes are most unusual even in a contemporary mosque design. Far from being the result of ignoring the past, however, a study of the mosque reveals a serious analysis of the numerous traditions of mosque architecture. The design also raises questions about the role of a mosque in the legislative complex of a country, which, since the 1920s, has had a majority Muslim population, but a secular system of government."[1] In fact dome and minaret are present in a truncated, stylized form so far from traditional shapes as to be almost unrecognizable. The glass *qibla* wall looking into a garden can be interpreted as an effort to connect worshippers to nature, an idea that is certainly not foreign to Islam, and yet, on the whole, the Ankara building breaks more rules than most religious buildings. Sitting somewhat below the Assembly buildings and purposefully aligned in the direction of Mecca, the stepped, largely blank building appears today to be rather closed and dated. According to the 1995 Award description: "The Jury believes that this new centre for worship is an important step in the development of a suitable architectural vocabulary for the design of contemporary mosques." As much as it confirms the success of the actual Mosque of the Grand National Assembly, the granting of the Aga Khan Award in the category 'Projects that Introduce Innovative Concepts Worthy of Attention' can be seen as an act of encouragement to the new solutions of the future.

1 Mohammad Al-Asad, 'The Mosque of the Turkish Grand National Assembly in Ankara: Breaking with Tradition', in: *Muqarnas: An Annual on the Visual Culture of the Islamic World*, XVI, 1999, pp. 155–168.

Another area that the Aga Khan Award for Architecture has sought to investigate is that of traditional building types such as the mosque. Although mosques can be created in informal spaces, there are certain rules of design that have been reinterpreted in the instance of the Ankara building. Local aesthetics also play a role in this case, raising the question of modernity and tradition in a particular way.

Menara Mesiniaga

KUALA LUMPUR, MALAYSIA

Architect: T. R. Hamzah and Yeang Sdn. Bhd.,
               Kuala Lumpur, Malaysia
Client: Mesiniaga Sdn. Bhd., Kuala Lumpur,
               Malaysia
Completed: 1992
               AKAA 1995 Cycle

■ A clear lesson of the ongoing Aga Khan Award for Architecture has been that the variety of work being done in Muslim countries is extraordinary. If the kind of low-cost housing encouraged by the Grameen Bank was singled out by the Award, so has the much more sophisticated type of architecture practised by Ken Yeang in Malaysia and elsewhere. An on-site project reviewer for the 1986 Cycle and a member of the 2007 Master Jury, Ken Yeang was born in 1948 in Penang, Malaysia. He attended the Architectural Association in London (1966–71) and Cambridge University (1971–75). Much of his subsequent work has been based on his Ph.D. dissertation at Cambridge on ecological design. He has worked with Tengku Robert Hamzah in the firm T. R. Hamzah & Yeang since 1976 in Kuala Lumpur. President of the Malaysian Institute of Architects from 1983 to 1986, his published works include *The Skyscraper, Bioclimatically Considered: A Design Primer* (AD, 1997). His Menara Mesiniaga, completed in 1992, is the headquarters of an IBM franchise in Subang Jaya on the outskirts of the Malaysian capital. This tower is a prototype of what the architect calls a "bioclimatic tall building." Two spirals of green "sky gardens" twist up the building and provide shade and visual contrast with the steel and aluminium surfaces. Core functions are placed on the warmer eastern side of the building and sunscreens permit a more frugal use of energy. As Peter Eisenman, a member of the 1995 Aga Khan Award Master Jury, said: "Here we have an example of a replicable corporate high-rise building that is environmentally sensitive to local discourse and is also forward looking."[1] Simply put, not everyone agrees that very tall buildings are a viable urban solution, and some architects, like Ken Yeang in Kuala Lumpur, have sought to improve at the very least the negative environmental impact that such buildings can have. The Award Master Jury, selecting this project under the category 'Projects that Address a Critical Architectural and Urbanistic Discourse', found that Yeang's building offered a viable alternative to "typical glass-enclosed air-conditioned medium-to-high-rise buildings." Ken Yeang has also succeeded in creating carefully crafted ecologically oriented buildings that are not at all unattractive. Confronting the equatorial climate of Kuala Lumpur with his prescient and persistent interest in 'green' design, Ken Yeang might well be said to be a pure product of his own country's pragmatic approach, where Muslims, Buddhists, Daoists, Hindus and Sikhs coexist in a usually progressive atmosphere. Malaysia's literacy rate exceeds eighty-eight per cent and Kuala Lumpur, with monuments like the soaring Petronas Towers (winner of a 2004 Aga Khan Award), is a symbol of regional modernity. Author of the recent National Library Board Building (Singapore, 2001–05) that includes over 6300 square metres of designated green space within the building, Ken Yeang is more than a figure of local interest. As his selection for the 1995 Award confirms, his thinking could well be applicable to many other areas of the world, Muslim or not. The lessons to be learned from his 'bioclimatically' designed structures are of interest wherever the consciousness of sustainability has progressed sufficiently to recognize that a 'green' building actually costs less than a wasteful counterpart.

1 Peter Eisenman, in: Cynthia C. Davidson and Ismaïl Serageldin (eds.), *Architecture Beyond Architecture*, London 1995.

The architect Ken Yeang has carefully studied the architecture of his country, Malaysia, and also the requirements of tall buildings in warm climates. His Menara Mesiniaga represents a concrete response to issues raised across broad parts of the world.

Tuwaiq Palace

RIYADH, SAUDI ARABIA

Architect:	OHO Joint Venture: Atelier Frei Otto; Buro Happold; Omrania Associates
Client:	Arriyadh Development Authority
Completed:	1985
	AKAA 1998 Cycle

■ The 1998 Master Jury that included the celebrated architects Zaha Hadid and Arata Isozaki gave only seven awards, selected from 424 nominated projects. As they said in their Report: "From the beginning of its deliberations, the Jury was concerned with recognizing projects that had a wider global context and meaning, as well as with identifying those projects that had regional relevance. It was also concerned not to duplicate messages conveyed through selections by earlier Juries, so that the absence of certain types of work needs to be understood in that spirit." Although the Aga Khan Award for Architecture has played a significant role in making many relatively small projects, which otherwise would

have been 'below the radar' of most members of the international architectural community, known, larger, truly successful buildings have sometimes proven more difficult to identify. The 1998 Jury Report points out that three of the projects it selected, "the Tuwaiq Palace, the Alhamra Arts Council and the Vidhan Bhavan were important and large-scale public buildings. Their form and context, within the Islamic world, was regarded by the Jury as very significant in the continuous process of evolving a contemporary architectural vocabulary. Their public functions and the relatively large scale of their volumes inevitably added to their importance as social catalysts within their societies." Intended to host "govern-

The originality of the Tuwaiq Palace lies in part in its combination of light and 'heavy' elements of tent-like structures and walls that enclose an oasis-like environment. Here, again, the question is one of adapting local traditions to current circumstances without indulging in pastiche.

The protected vegetal environment of the interior precinct emphasizes the idea of refuge from a desert environment, and highlights the connection to ancient ways of life in the region.

ment functions, state receptions and cultural festivals that introduce Saudi arts and customs to the international community, and vice versa," the Tuwaiq Palace makes clear and present reference to two local, traditional structural types – tents and fortresses. Named after a nearby mountain, it is the main cultural facility for the diplomatic community in Riyadh and is located on the north-western side of the city, facing the Wadi Hanifa. With its curving 800-metre-long, twelve-metre-high enclosure wall, the structure has also been compared to a desert oasis, particularly because of the lush inner gardens that participate in the twisting, spiralling patterns of the architecture and contrast with the largely arid exterior. In an unusual twist on the type of architectural competition which led to this design, the client asked the two winning firms, Omrania and Atelier Frei Otto (with Buro Happold) to work together on the final scheme. Within the reinforced-concrete walls covered with local limestone, which were part of the Omrania proposal, tensile structures, double-skinned Teflon-coated woven fibre tents, designed with the participation of the noted German engineer Frei Otto, enclose lounges, reception areas, restaurants and a café. With the exception of the Riyadh limestone on the walls, the materials and technology for the entire project were imported, but the representative of the client, Dr Mohammed al-Sheikh, played

an important role in forming the final concept. The Jury singled out the building for its "architectural qualities and its setting within a dramatic landscape, the idea of a soft fortification, its hard and soft spaces, and its combination of concrete, stone, tensile structures and landscaping." Given its choice of materials and its design, the Tuwaiq Palace takes into account both local culture and climate while offering an innovative combination of massive walls and the extremely light tensile structures of Frei Otto.

With pools, courtyards and large arched openings, the Palace and its internal landscaping seem to emerge from the existing site without any falsely archaic overtone. The connection between the past and the present, and above all to the region, is clearly established.

Kahere Eila Poultry Farming School

KOLIAGBE, GUINEA

Architect:	Heikkinen-Komonen Architects
Patron:	Eila Kivekäs
Client:	Centre Avicole Kahere, Indigo Development Association
Completed:	2000
	AKAA 2001 Cycle

■ Eight Awards were given in 2001 by the Master Jury of the Eighth Cycle (1999–2001). Like previous groups, the Jury involved in these selections was varied both in terms of origins and of intellectual background. Aside from the architects Darab Diba (Iran), Ricardo Legorreta (Mexico), Glenn Murcutt (Australia) and Raj Rewal (India), there was also a philosopher (Abdou Filali-Ansari), an archaeologist (Zahi Hawass), a sociologist (Norani Othman) and an artist (Mona Hatoum). The Jury Report underlines that "some of the projects are organized to encourage disadvantaged communities to advance their conditions by increasing productivity, improving their built environment and sharing access to modern culture and communication. Joint efforts by people who benefit from the modern economy and those who have remained in rural conditions have made it possible to reverse the constant flow of migration and the concomitant depletion of local human resources and deterioration of environmental and living conditions. Some projects respond to educational needs, such as preserving the life and culture of an ancient civilization, while others provide instruction in techniques of animal production to enrich diet and nutrition."

Measuring just 340 square metres and having cost only USD 104,000, the Kahere Eila Poultry Farming School was one winner of the Eighth Cycle that fits this description well. The Finnish architects, surely better known for their large-scale work in Scandinavia, also completed a Village Health Centre (Mali, Guinea, 1994), two village schools and the Villa Eila (Mali, Guinea, 1995), working with Eila Kivekäs (1931–99). Their involvement in the Poultry Farming School is in part due to the intervention of the development aid organization Indigo, in collaboration with the Finnish Poultry Farmers' Associ-

ation, which have supported the development of chicken farming in Guinea. The Kahere School includes a classroom for twelve students, a student dormitory and a teacher's house grouped around a square courtyard. Construction was carried out with stabilized earth bricks made in a manual press. Double brick walls were erected in the school to provide thermodynamic insulation, and good airflow through the complex was a goal of the architects.

The Master Jury citation explains the choice of the Poultry Farming School in the following terms: "This project has received an Award because it draws on traditional local planning relationships, with a courtyard dominated by a central tree articulating teaching and accommodation spaces. The complex is adjusted to the conditions of the tropical climate: technologies are simple, including locally made stabilized earth-blocks, woven split-cane panel ceilings, and pigmented concrete floors and roof tiles. Sophisticated structural elements – columns and trusses – are made of composite timber and metal, strengthening the materials available to local craftsmen. The architecture uses a deceptively simple language and is distinguished by clarity of form and appropriateness of scale. The solution is a fine example of an elegantly humble yet modern architecture that successfully crosses the boundaries of local Guinean and Nordic traditions and, in the process, avoids mimicry."

The Finnish architects involved in this project might not have seemed the most obvious choice to build in a tropical environment, and yet they have readily taken up the challenge of combining local planning tradition and their knowledge of spare architectural form, not unrelated to Nordic thinking, with the needs of a rural community.

The search for simple
housing designs
that employ readily
available materials
is one of great
importance in the
developing world.
The use of sandbags
and barbed wire to
hold them together
is intellectually
appealing here, as
well as conceivably
practical.

Sandbag Shelter Prototypes

VARIOUS LOCATIONS

Architect: Cal-Earth Institute, Nader Khalili,
                    United States
First Development: 1992
                    AKAA 2004 Cycle

■ Nader Khalili was born in 1937 in Iran and trained as an architect in Turkey and the United States. From 1970 to 1975, he practised architecture in Iran, and has since dedicated himself to research on building with earth. Khalili founded the California Institute of Earth Art and Architecture (Cal-Earth) in Hesperia, California, in 1986, and has been directing the Architectural Research Programme at SCI-Arc in Los Angeles since 1982. Khalili basically found that stacking sandbags in circular plans to form domed structures, with barbed wire laid between each row to prevent the bags from shifting, was a way of providing readily available and stable housing. His prototypes received California building permits and have also met the requirements of the United Nations High Commissioner for Refugees (UNHCR) for emergency housing. Both the UNHCR and the United Nations Development Programme (UNDP) used the system in 1995 to provide temporary shelters for a flood of refugees coming into Iran from Iraq. The 2004 Master Jury made up of Ghada Amer (artist), Hanif Kara (structural engineer), Rahul Mehrotra (architect and urban planner), Farshid Moussavi (architect), Modjtaba Sadria (philosopher), Reinhard Schulze (philosopher), Elías Torres Tur (architect and landscape architect), Billie Tsien (architect) and Jafar Tukan (architect) had some disagreements about this project, with some Jury members feeling that the scheme was impractical and unlikely to be used widely, while others felt that it was important to encourage research of this nature.

The Jury citation reads in part: "These shelters serve as a prototype for temporary housing using extremely inexpensive means to provide safe homes that can be built quickly and have the high insulation values necessary in arid climates. Their curved form was devised in response to seismic conditions, ingeniously using sand or earth as raw materials, since their flexibility allows the construction of single- and double-curvature compression shells that can withstand lateral seismic forces … The prototype is a symbiosis of tradition and technology. It employs vernacular forms, integrating load-bearing and tensile structures, but provides a remarkable degree of strength and durability for this type of construction, which is traditionally weak and fragile, through a composite system of sandbags and barbed wire."

Despite whatever impracticality the Master Jury might have seen in this project, or even the fact that the shelters have not actually been used or inhabited widely, it does address the very substantial problems of homeless people subsequent to natural disasters or more human-made catastrophes. Their simplicity and seismic resistance, coupled with the fact that they make use of the very symbols of war and conflict (barbed wire and sandbags), make them potentially much more significant for large, disfavoured populations than any computer-modelled piece of contemporary architecture.

Concentric placement of the sandbags results in this instance in an almost traditional looking architectural environment, with a dome and an overhead oculus.

Petronas Towers

KUALA LUMPUR, MALAYSIA

Architect:	Cesar Pelli & Associates, United States
Client:	Kuala Lumpur City Centre Holdings Sdn. Bhd., Malaysia
Completed:	1997–99
	AKAA 2004 Cycle

■ Cesar Pelli, born in Tucuman, Argentina, in 1926, might not seem to be one of the most likely architects to receive an Aga Khan Award, particularly since his experience of building in Muslim countries is limited. Pelli immigrated to the United States and worked for ten years in the office of Eero Saarinen. The major buildings designed by Pelli with his different firms – DMJM, Gruen Associates, and Cesar Pelli & Associates – amount to one of the most prestigious lists of any practising architect. These include the Pacific Design Centre in Los Angeles (1975), the tower expansion of the Museum of Modern Art in New York (1977), the World Financial Centre in New York (1980–88) and the Canary Wharf Tower in London (1987–91). Recipient of the 1995 AIA Gold Medal, Pelli was the winner of the 1991 competition for this project. To meet the demand for urban growth of the Malaysian capital, the Selangor Turf Club and its surrounding land, some thirty-nine hectares in the heart of the commercial district or "Golden Triangle", were freed for the construction of a new "city within a city", the Kuala Lumpur City Centre (KLCC). The twin eighty-eight-storey, 452-metre-high Petronas Towers are connected by a sky bridge at the forty-first floor to facilitate inter-tower communication and traffic. Boasting a GDP growth of 8.4% in 1994 when these towers were under construction, Malaysia's economy remains one of the fastest expanding in the world and the Petronas Towers marked Kuala Lumpur as a centre to be reckoned with. The Master Jury wrote: "This project has received an Award because it represents a new direction in skyscraper design, featuring advanced technology while symbolizing local and national aspirations. The project embodies several innovations, ranging from the use of unusually high-strength concrete to facilitate a soft-tube structural system to an inventive vertical transportation concept and the integration of cutting-edge energy con-

servation systems. The success of this project lies in the manner in which it incorporates these technological innovations while generating a slender form that responds poetically to the broader landscape. The simple geometrical pattern that generates the plan not only uses space efficiently to maximize exposure to natural light, but also creates a rich spatial expression. The building has become an icon that expresses the sophistication of contemporary Malaysian society and builds on the country's rich traditions to shape a world city."

The choice of the Petronas Towers amongst the winners of the 2004 Aga Khan Award winners takes on a particular significance when viewed from the point of view of the deliberations of the Steering Committee and Master Jury. A number of 2004 Master Jury members felt strongly that the Award should have a more "contemporary" or possibly more forward-looking emphasis than had been the case up to that point. The Steering Committee argued successfully that it would be a strong signal to hold an Award ceremony in a contemporary urban location as opposed to the more historic venues previously selected for these events. Thus, the Petronas Towers were chosen for the remittal of the 2007 Awards.

Though designed by the Argentine-American architect Cesar Pelli, the Petronas Towers in Kuala Lumpur represent a significant step onto the world stage by a largely Muslim city. Occupying a central location in the city, they are symbolic of the emergence of Malaysia as an economic power.

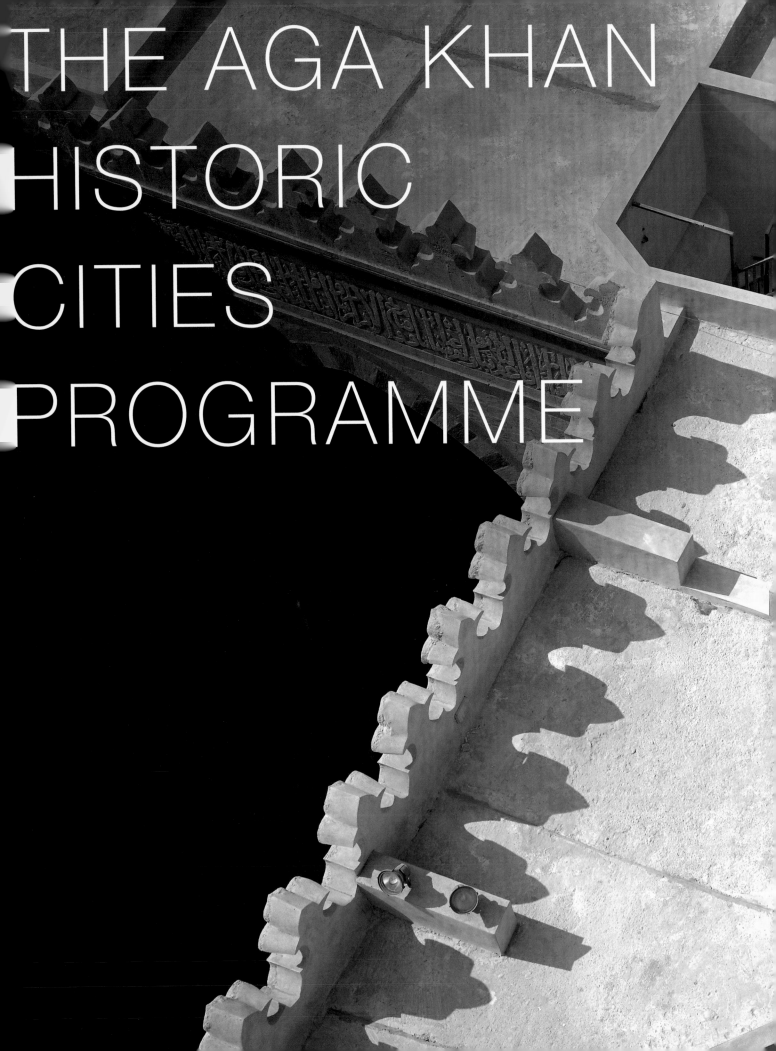

THE AGA KHAN
HISTORIC
CITIES
PROGRAMME

The Aga Khan Historic Cities Programme

Created in 1991, the Aga Khan Historic Cities Programme (AKHCP)[1] is a branch of the Aga Khan Trust for Culture that was until spring 2006 under the leadership of Stefano Bianca and is now directed by Cameron Rashti. Although some restoration work (Zafra House, Granada, 1991) had been carried out earlier under the Aga Khan Award for Architecture, once established in the early 1990s the AKHCP provided a dedicated team of professionals and a methodology and policy that enabled exemplary restoration, urban and environmental planning, and construction projects across the Muslim world. The recent Azhar Park in Cairo, which includes new architecture and landscape design, as well as historic preservation work and other aspects (see the following pages), is a measure of the scale and success of AKHCP projects. As described by the organization itself: "The Aga Khan Historic Cities Programme (AKHCP) undertakes conservation, restoration and adaptive reuse of significant monuments in Islamic countries in the context of wider area development projects which aim at integrated and holistic rehabilitation of selected urban districts or developing rural areas. Together with conservation, Aga Khan Historic Cities Programme projects focus on the operation and maintenance aspects of completed restoration projects, to keep historic buildings alive and ensure their sustainability. Moreover, the Programme engages in the revitalization of the traditional urban fabric around landmark buildings, including housing, social facilities and public open spaces. Through collateral activities, the Aga Khan Historic Cities Programme contributes to the improvement of socio-economic living conditions in the project area and beyond, mobilizes local awareness and participation, and assists in local capacity- and institution-building. So far, the Programme has been – and for the moment continues to be – active in northern Pakistan (Hunza and Baltistan), Cairo, Zanzibar, Samarkand, Delhi, Mostar, Aleppo and other sites in Syria, as well as in Kabul, Herat and Mopti."

In Cairo, Kabul and elsewhere, the Aga Khan Historic Cities Programme has increasingly participated in a multiple approach together with other Aga Khan organizations that form the Aga Khan Development Network (AKDN), such as the Aga Khan Fund for Economic Development (AKFED) and the Tourism Promotion Services (TPS) that controls the Serena Hotels and Inns. The goal of ongoing AKHCP/AKDN interventions is never to simply restore a building and then leave; rather, a much more profound impact is sought. In 2005, referring to initiatives in Afghanistan, the Aga Khan stated: "It is heartening that a recent external evaluation, commissioned by the World Bank, found this AKDN approach innovative and effective in forming credible, legitimate and self-reliant institutions. The report commended the outcome as a significant contribution to democratic governance and civil society development in the country. This observation corresponds to our experience in many countries, similar to that of the United Nations, that a healthy civil society is indispensable to fostering and legitimizing pluralism which itself is the foundation of democratic government. This remains a paramount challenge ... Our experience in situations as diverse as remote parts of northern Pakistan, to Delhi, Zanzibar and central Cairo, is that the restoration of historic communities and important cultural assets serves as a trampoline for economic development. The restoration activity is a source of direct employment for workers and skilled craftsmen, many of whom live in adjacent neighbourhoods. The refurbished facilities themselves become an attraction for tourists, generating more opportunity. And as the residents of surrounding areas find themselves with new sources of income, they spend some of it improving their own homes and neighbourhoods."[2]

And yet even this broad picture of the activities of the Aga Khan, frequently spearheaded by the Historic Cities Programme, does not paint the full picture of the underlying goals. The success of a local programme in creating jobs, pride and sustainable development is certainly laudable, but it does not necessarily speak to the even greater problems that separate the Muslim world from the West. In 2003, the Aga Khan declared: "In the troubled times in which we live, it is important to remember, and honour, a vision of a pluralistic society. Tolerance, openness and understanding toward other peoples' cultures, social structures, values and faiths are now essential to the very survival of an interdependent world. Pluralism is no longer simply an asset or a prerequisite for progress and development, it is vital to our existence. Never perhaps more so than at the present time must we renew with vigour our creative engagement in revitalizing shared heritage through collaborative ventures such as the project we are inaugurating today."[3] Many of the locations where the AKHCP has intervened, such as Zanzibar or Kabul, are rich in history and architecture precisely because they have been located at the crossroads between civilizations. Rather than in any sense rejecting the implicit cross-fertilization of cultures, the Aga Khan clearly embraces the pluralism which he sees as "vital to our existence." The Aga Khan Historic Cities Programme thus has a mission to build bridges between the past and the present, but also between cultures and civilizations.

Some of the projects undertaken by the Historic Cities Programme are briefly outlined on the following pages.

1 The Aga Khan Historic Cities Programme (AKHCP) was originally named the Historic Cities Support Programme (HCSP).
2 Speech by His Highness the Aga Khan at the opening of the Kabul Serena Hotel, 8 November 2005.
3 Speech by His Highness the Aga Khan at the ceremony to inaugurate the restored Humayun's Tomb Gardens, New Delhi, 15 April 2003.

Azhar Park

CAIRO, EGYPT

Architect / Planner:	Aga Khan Trust for Culture; Aga Khan Cultural Services (AKCS-E); Sasaki Associates; Sites International Landscape Architects
Funding Agency:	Aga Khan Trust for Culture
Owner:	Cairo Governorate
Date of Intervention:	1997 for site access, start of enabling works and master grading; 2000 for all other construction contracts
Completed:	2004

Right, an aerial view of Azhar Park shows the Hilltop Restaurant in the foreground and the Lakeside Café at the top of the image.

Below, a general view of about 1880 of Cairo, Egypt, looking north-north-west from the Muqattam Hills shows the Citadel (eastern half), with the Darassa rubbish dump and the Darb al-Ahmar district visible in the centre-right. The Fatimid 11th-century al-Juyushi Mosque is visible lower left. Unsigned. Courtesy of the Fine Arts Library, Harvard College Library.

■ In 1984, the Aga Khan Award for Architecture organized an international seminar entitled 'The Expanding Metropolis: Coping with the Urban Growth of Cairo'. During that year, the Aga Khan met Hassan Fathy in the architect's apartment on the top floor of an eighteenth-century urban mansion called Beit al-Fann, in the area of the Citadel, close to the Mosque of Sultan Hasan. From the terrace of Fathy's apartment, the monuments of Islamic Cairo were clearly visible, but so too was an empty area running along the remains of the Ayyubid Walls, built in the twelfth and thirteenth centuries by Salah al-Din and his successors. The land was vacant because it had served since the late Mamluk period[1] as the city's rubbish dump. More than five centuries of refuse, in places over

forty-five-metres deep, had all but engulfed the historic walls. Two years later, the thirty-hectare site on the Darassa Hills belonging to the Governate of the city was selected for the creation of Azhar Park, one of the most ambitious and far-reaching projects undertaken by the Aga Khan.

Within clear view of the Citadel, Azhar Park is adjacent to Khayrbek Mosque near both the Sultan Hasan Mosque and *madrasa* built for Sultan Hasan bin Mohammad bin Qala'un in 1256 and the Aqsunqur, or Blue Mosque, built by one of al-Nasir Muhammad's Emirs, Shams al-Din Aqsunqur, in 1346. A more recent monument visible from the Park on the same axis as the Sultan Hasan Mosque is the Rifa'i Mosque designed by Mustapha Fahmi at the order of Khushyar, mother of the Khedive Ismail, and

Right, an aerial view of Azhar Park in Cairo, Egypt, shows the restored Ayyubid Wall with the Darb al-Ahmar district to the left.

Below, the plan is rotated 90° vis-à-vis the aerial photograph and shows the Wall marking the transition from the Park to the neighbourhood at the top.

completed in 1912 by Max Herz Pasha. The Park is named after the great al-Azhar Mosque, located slightly to the north of the neighbouring al-Darb al-Ahmar area. Al-Azhar was created by Jawhar the Sicilian, Fatimid founder of Cairo just after his conquest in 970. Al-Azhar, meaning "the most flourishing and shining" in Arabic, was dedicated to Sayeda Fatima al-Zahra', daughter of the Prophet Mohammed, from whom His Highness the Aga Khan descends. It is thus in the heart of Islamic Cairo that the Aga Khan stood in the completed Park in 2005 and declared: "Twenty-one years ago we had a vision that launched us on a journey of inquiry, exploration and discovery that took us through some one thousand years of history of this extraordinary city."[2]

Turning the dusty, uninhabited sediment of Cairo into a living park was a task of vast proportions involving many people. Project leaders such as Stefano Bianca and Cameron Rashti of the Aga Khan Historic Cities Programme (AKHCP) led the way, but the architects and landscape designers formed Azhar Park as it exists today. Maher Stino and Laila Elmasry Stino of Sites International assumed the task of the landscape design after the essentially axial layout, pointing toward the Citadel in particular, was conceived by the Watertown (Massachu-

setts) firm Sasaki Associates. Much of the peripheral architecture of the Park (kiosks, administrative offices, and so on) was designed by Maher Stino and his group, who are based in Cairo. "We have sixteen million people," he declared while working on the project, "and we have almost no open space – nothing. We want to help the public understand what a park is and how to appreciate plants and nature. We also want something unique to Cairo. We do not want a copy of London's Regent's Park." Limestone-block retaining walls that call on the expertise of local masons are a recurring element throughout the design and great attention has been paid to the particularities of the site, where water supply and run-off are sensitive issues. On the eastern side, where the topography is given to gentle slopes and there are no neighbouring residential areas, a design with large grass areas and flowers gives an oasis-like feeling of freshness and greenery. But the steeper western facade, near al-Darb al-Ahmar and the Ayyubid Wall, posed the problem of potential water accumulation and was thus planted with more desert varieties, including cacti whose seeds were brought from Arizona by project horticulturalist El-Saady Mohamed Badawy. Numerous fountains, especially near the two restaurants, recall the traditions of the

ant, inspired by Fatimid and Mamluk building traditions. Rami El Dahan has since gone on to design the new Ismaili Centre in Dubai, another arched, stone building (see page 190).

Summing up the intervention, AKHCP's present director, Cameron Rashti, explains: "While excluded from the historic city, the proximity and size of the park site have in recent years posed a dilemma for would-be occupants. The disadvantages of its geo-technical properties have been significant enough to create a quasi 'frontier' to urban growth, while its proximity to the historic core and offer of large open space has made it a natural zone for transformation, and the opportunities to transform Cairo's edges have not gone unnoticed in the last few decades." As the Aga Khan explained in his inaugural speech, creating this great new green space in the heart of Cairo was not all that his organizations undertook, because "what started as one project actually turned into three: the design and construction of a park, the restoration of the Ayyubid Wall, and the community redevelopment of the historically important al-Darb al-Ahmar neighbourhood. All," he concluded, "are tightly interconnected and have added to the body of knowledge we can share with others."[4]

1 The Burji Mamluks ruled Egypt until their defeat by the Ottoman Turks in 1517 under Selim I.
2 Speech by His Highness the Aga Khan at the inauguration of Azhar Park, Cairo, Egypt, 25 March 2005.
3 Résidence Andalous, Sousse, Tunisia, 1980. Architects: Serge Santelli and Cabinet GERAU (M. Cherif). Client: Consortium Tuniso-Kowëitien de Développement.
4 Speech by His Highness the Aga Khan at the inauguration of Azhar Park, Cairo, Egypt, 25 March 2005.

Islamic garden, but here, too, Maher Stino avoids direct citations, preferring to allow modernity to be the guiding rule. The very scale of the landscape and horticulture effort speaks of the courage and will necessary to turn these hills into a real contemporary garden. 1.5 million cubic metres of rubble and soil, the equivalent of more than 80,000 truckloads, were moved to accomplish the task and more than 655,000 plants and trees now grow where the Aga Khan saw only barren mounds of refuse in 1984.

The two restaurants in the park were designed respectively by the Egyptian architects Rami El Dahan with Soheir Farid, and the French architect Serge Santelli. Winner of an Aga Khan Award for Architecture in the Second Cycle,[3] Santelli created the Lakeside Café, while Dahan fashioned the more substantial Hilltop Restaur-

Pictures of Azhar Park show its central location in Islamic Cairo, with the Citadel in the distance. The aerial view top left shows the site before the intervention of the Aga Khan. As the images imply, the Park has come today to be considered a veritable oasis in the city for many residents.

Views of the Hilltop
Restaurant in Azhar
Park, Cairo, by Rami
El Dahan with Soheir
Farid. Calling on
Fatimid tradition,
the architecture is
intended to respond
both to its location
and to the history of
the Egyptian capital.

The Lakeside Café in Azhar Park, Cairo, by French architect Serge Santelli strikes a somewhat more modern note than the Hilltop Restaurant. It is situated on an artificial lake created to assist with the irrigation of the Park itself.

Al-Darb al-Ahmar Projects

CAIRO, EGYPT

Architect/Planner:	Aga Khan Trust for Culture; Aga Khan Cultural Services AKCS-E
Funding Agency:	Aga Khan Trust for Culture; Social Fund for Development of Egypt; Egyptian Swiss Development Fund; Ford Foundation; World Monuments Fund; Italian Ministry of Foreign Affairs; Aga Khan Agency for Microfinance; US State Department
Owner:	Ministry of Awkaf
Date of Intervention:	2000
Completed:	ongoing

■ The work of the Aga Khan's organizations in the Darb al-Ahmar district of Cairo, located near the former Ayyubid Wall and Azhar Park, "encompasses an extensive social development programme, including apprenticeship arrangements, housing rehabilitation, microcredit and health care facilities. Several mosques, old palaces, historic houses and public open spaces are being rehabilitated in an effort to make them accessible to

Views of the Darb al-Ahmar district in Cairo, Egypt. The aerial picture to the right was taken during restoration work on the Ayyubid Wall, visible, together with a green band inside Azhar Park, at the bottom of the photograph.

Work carried out by the AKHCP in al-Darb al-Ahmar, including the training of local craftsmen and assistance given to workshops.

Right, the Khayrbek Mosque complex in Cairo, Egypt, being restored.

the local community and visitors. The most prominent of these are the sixteenth-century Khayrbek Mosque with the adjacent *sabil kuttab* and an attached eighteenth-century house, the fourteenth-century Alin Aq Palace, the Umm al-Sultan Shaaban Mosque and *madrasa* and Aslam Square." Housing rehabilitation activities undertaken by the Aga Khan Trust for Culture in the area averaged about fifty houses per year through 2007 and a housing credit plan has also assisted individuals in rehabilitating their own homes.

Stefano Bianca, former head of the Aga Khan Historic Cities Programme (AKHCP), outlines the unusual multi-pronged, ongoing nature of the intervention of the organizations of the Aga Khan, and others, in the Darb-al-Ahmar district of Cairo in terms of seven related priorities:

1 Architectural Analysis. The morphology of the historic urban form, in most cases 'organically' grown over many centuries, must be recorded, analyzed and creatively interpreted to provide a suitable framework not only for conservation, but also for careful repair and substitution of individual components, whenever needed.

2 Appropriate Planning Technologies. Sustainable ways of introducing modern infrastructure must be assessed, and existing tools and techniques must be adapted in order to provide an optimum level of viability without disrupting the essential features of the historic urban form.

3 Improvement of Housing Conditions. Introducing or improving water supply, sewerage and electricity networks is essential, but requires the corresponding networks to be adjusted to the constraints of the given urban form and the particular housing typology.

4 Public Open Space Improvement. Often public open spaces – whether streets, squares or barren land – are neglected because they are seen as residual spaces unrelated to responsible social groups or individuals. Re-establishing a sense of ownership and responsibility by involving the local community in corresponding upgrading projects is a tool to foster civic pride and solidarity.

5 Conservation and Adaptive Reuse of Historic Buildings. When funding is short, it may not always be possible to conserve or restore the complete architectural heritage. Priority must be given to projects that can foster a sense of ownership and solidarity in the local community, and that can become catalysts for corollary urban conservation and renewal processes.

6 Socio-Economic Development. Raising existing living standards is essential in order to back up parallel conservation and rehabilitation projects and to ensure that local communities stand behind the overall rehabilitation effort.

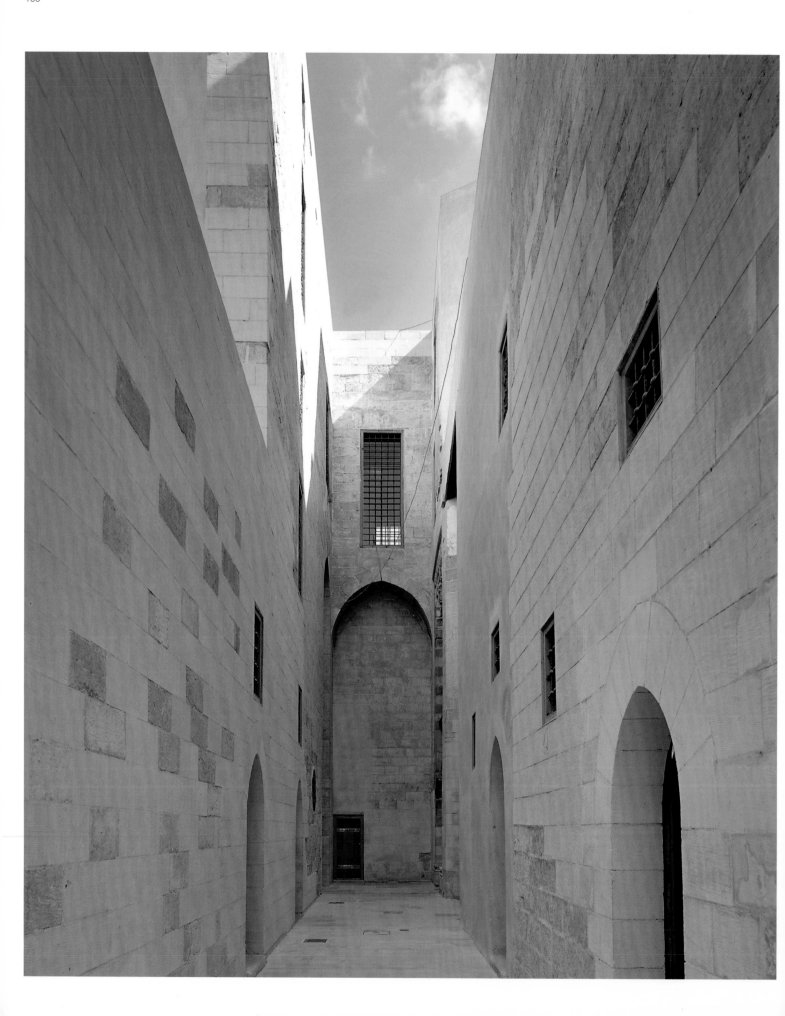

7 Institutional Support. An appropriate local institutional system has to be built up (or strengthened) in order to coordinate, drive and sustain the rehabilitation efforts, drawing both on internal resources and external contributions and incentives.[1]

Although it was until recent years a centre for the drug trade, the Darb al-Ahmar district is home to a deeply rooted community. Approximately 200,000 people, many of them related by marriage, live and work in this area where real unemployment rates may not be as high as estimates imply. Studies done by the AKCS-E showed that contrary to many assumptions the population of al-Darb al-Ahmar consists mostly of people born in the area (72%) with only seven per cent having been born outside Cairo. Their illiteracy rate (19%) is lower than the Egyptian urban average (26%), and the male unemployment rate was about eighteen per cent before the opening of the Park. Household income, on average USD 1052 per year (based on the exchange rate of LE 4.65 to the US dollar in June 2002) appears to be considerably lower than known averages for the city of Cairo, USD 2570 in 1993, when the exchange rate was then LE 3.50 to the US dollar.[2] As the AKHCP explains: "The Azhar Park Project is a catalyst for social, economic and cultural renewal and improvement and will have far-reaching consequences for the residents of the neighbouring al-Darb al-Ahmar district." The obvious fact that the residents of the area live in the very heart of Cairo, and not at its abandoned edge, has been underlined not only by the historic preservation work done on the Ayyubid Wall and within the community, but also by the creation of the highly symbolic park at their doorstep. Rather than living in squalor as was largely the case before the interventions of the organizations of the Aga Khan, the residents of al-Darb-al-Ahmar have been offered a place in Cairo's future.

1 Stefano Bianca, in: Stefano Bianca and Philip Jodidio (eds.), *Cairo, Revitalising a Historic Metropolis*, Turin 2004.
2 'El-Darb El-Ahmar Neighbourhood Conservation Planning', AKCS-E, Bab Al-Wazeer Area, social survey of 840 inhabitants conducted in June 2002 by Dina K. Shehayeb.

Top, the restored interior of the mosque/*madrasa* of Umm al-Sultan Shaaban, Cairo, Egypt, and left, its entrance corridor.

Above, the restored interior of Khayrbek Mosque, Cairo, Egypt.

Ayyubid Wall

CAIRO, EGYPT

Architect/Planner:	Aga Khan Trust for Culture; Aga Khan Cultural Services (AKCS-E)
Funding Agency:	Aga Khan Trust for Culture
Owner:	Supreme Council of Antiquities
Date of Intervention:	1999
Completed:	2007

■ Francesco Siravo recalls that the construction of the Ayyubid Wall "was begun in 1176 by Salah al-Din, a Kurd of the Ayyubid clan who came to Cairo from Syria and overthrew the Fatimid caliphate in 1171. Salah al-Din's fortifications were built to contain Cairo, his citadel and the pre-Fatimid settlements (Fustat, al-Askar and al-Qata'i) within a single system."[1] With the expansion of the city, these walls were rendered useless and the present area of Azhar Park turned over to refuse beginning in the sixteenth century. The proud walls gradually disappeared under the accumulated debris of the city, but it was along this line that the edge of the new Park was determined, with the largely run-down area of al-Darb al-Ahmar just beyond. In fact, through the centuries, al-Darb al-Ahmar encroached on the wall itself in some places, with buildings rising from its stones. Although it was not originally part of the AKTC scheme for Azhar Park, it became apparent in the course of the work that an effort to excavate and renovate at least part of the fortifications would make eminent good sense. A length of approximately 1500 metres from Bab al-Wazir to al-Azhar Street, forming the boundary between the Darb al-Ahmar district and the Park, was thus completely unearthed and restored. The 'Philosophy and Guidelines for Intervention' outlined by the Aga Khan Historic Cities Programme (AKHCP) for work on the Eastern Ayyubid Wall makes clear the careful respect for the site and for international conventions that was a basis for the work. "The methodologies and guidelines offered in this report are designed to achieve maximum integrity of the wall with the least possible physical intervention. The importance of place, as expressed by cultural value and significance, and a respect for history as continuous change are critical to the future development and continued life of the wall and neighbourhood. Altogether,

these proposals advocate the conservation and integration of the Ayyubid Wall within the traditional urban fabric and contemporary life of al-Darb al-Ahmar, as well as the provision of tourist opportunities of the city's fortifications to park visitors."[2] It should be noted in passing that alternative schemes would have involved the removal of the slums and workshops of al-Darb al-Ahmar and its conversion into an open-air museum of sorts. The intervention of the AKTC in al-Darb al-Ahmar obviously does not espouse the view of the historic area as "open-air museum." Rather, a substantial effort has been made to reintegrate monuments as complex as the long-buried

Right, an aerial view showing restoration work on the Ayyubid Wall with Azhar Park to the left of the image.

Left, directly next to the Wall, the new Darb Shoughlan Community Centre, another AKHCP project in Cairo, Egypt.

Right, a sweeping view of the restored Wall looking from the Park toward al-Darb al-Ahmar, Cairo, Egypt.

Below, an interior view of a tower in the Ayyubid Wall.

Ayyubid Wall into the life of the community. This was done not only by opening connections into the new Azhar Park, but also by renewing housing and monuments that abut the Wall or even sit partially on top of it at one point. And rather than seeking to move residents and local workshops to some distant new location, this project takes on the training of local craftsmen in the traditional arts of carpentry and stonework that they no longer fully master. Rather than being considered as a barrier between al-Darb al-Ahmar and the new Park, the Ayyubid Wall, thanks to the organizations of the Aga Khan, has in a sense been reintegrated as a living part of the city and a true sense of historic continuity has been created between Islamic Cairo's past and its future.

1 Francesco Siravo, in: Stefano Bianca and Philip Jodidio (eds.), *Cairo, Revitalising a Historic Metropolis*, Turin 2004.
2 Historic Cities Support Programme, Technical Brief no. 4, 'The Eastern Ayyubid Wall of Cairo'.

Restoration of Baltit Fort

KARIMABAD, NORTHERN AREAS,
PAKISTAN

Architect/Planner:	Aga Khan Trust for Culture; Aga Khan Cultural Services (AKCS-P)
Funding Agency:	Aga Khan Trust for Culture; Government of Norway; Japanese Embassy (in Islamabad); Swiss Development Cooperation (SDC); Getty Grant Foundation; Spanish, German, Greek and French Embassies (in Islamabad); Sumitomo Foundation; American Express International
Owner:	Baltit Heritage Fund
Date of Intervention:	1992
Completed:	1996

■ Richard Hughes, a conservation engineer who worked on the restoration of Baltit Fort in the Hunza Valley in the Northern Areas of Pakistan, describes the site as "the most rugged area in the world," in the midst of the Karakoram Mountains, with thirty-two mountain peaks ranging from 5500 to 7500 metres in height within 100 kilometres. He says: "Prior to the late 1960s, there was no access to the region and tracking overland on foot from the villages of Gilgit to Baltit used to take up to four days." The Fort sits above the town of Karimabad (formerly Baltit) renamed for His Highness the Aga Khan. According to the surveys done on the structure, which had fallen into disrepair, construction occurred over a period of 700 years in seventy distinct phases. As reported by Hughes and fellow consultant Didier Lefort: "When visited in 1979, Baltit Fort seemed a labyrinth of dark, smelly and dusty rooms. All the roofs were decayed and pierced by holes, renders were full of cracks and walls were leaning precariously outside the foundation lines. Yet the fort had an undeniably unique and distinctive character. The massive structure remained delicately poised on top of the soil cliff, and revealed wood construction detailing purposely arranged to better resist earthquakes. The archaeological value of the site and structure was important, yielding strong evidence of a continuous historical past and very little evidence of modernity. More importantly, the building still dominated and controlled contemporary life in Karimabad and Hun-

za."[1] Before restoration work on the Fort could begin, its ownership was generously transferred from Ghazanfar Ali Khan II, a descendent of the Mirs of Hunza, to a new public foundation, the Baltit Heritage Trust. A programme calling for reuse of the Fort as a museum was approved and complementary funding obtained from the Getty Grant Foundation in 1991. Five years of intensive restoration work using both modern and traditional methods and numerous locally trained workers and young Pakistani architects, often from the Northern Areas, have allowed the Baltit Fort to return to its former splendour as a museum and cultural centre receiving as many as 20,000 visitors a year. The first project carried out by the Aga Khan Historic Cities Programme, the exemplary Baltit Fort restoration has encouraged other revitalization efforts in Karimabad and proven the value of carefully planned, ongoing interventions. In a 27 June 2005 issue, *Time Magazine* dubbed the project "the most amazing fort ever rebuilt."

1 Historic Cities Support Programme, 'Conservation and Development in Hunza and Baltistan'.

The restored Baltit Fort against the dramatic background of the Karakoram Mountains in the Northern Areas of Pakistan.

Left, the former Queen's apartment on the first floor of Baltit Fort; this space is now used to exhibit traditional wooden furniture and utensils.

Right, the restored Baltit Fort with the western bay window on the facade in evidence, the interior of which is shown lower left.

Ganish Village Projects

CENTRAL HUNZA, NORTHERN AREAS,
PAKISTAN

Architect / Planner:	Aga Khan Trust for Culture; Aga Khan Cultural Services (AKCS-P)
Date of Intervention:	1996
Completed:	2002

■ The success of the work of the Aga Khan Trust for Culture in Karimabad led to other projects in the area. As Masood Khan, a planning consultant working in the area, writes: "The Aga Khan Historic Cities Programme community-based village planning and rehabilitation efforts in Karimabad … have had an effect far beyond their immediate area of application. Other villages in the area, such as Altit and Ganish, realized the positive change achieved and requested similar types of assistance from the AKCS-P and its donors, in particular NORAD (Norwegian Development Agency) and the Japanese Embassy."[1] Ganish, located on a plateau on the edge of the main river gorge, and Altit are two other original settlements in the Hunza Valley. The old village of Ganish contains approximately thirty-two houses built in the traditional Hunza style. The main ceremonial and public space of the town called the *jataq* is surrounded by four wooden mosques, but the use of the space had been abandoned and the mosques were in an advanced state of dilapidation. As Masood Khan points out, however, "the village elders were conscious of the assets of their village. They knew of its ancient past and had a notion of the value of its heritage. This was an authentic traditional village untouched by bad repair or alterations and endowed with a rich mixture of traditional urban spaces, defensive structures and religious and residential architecture of considerable artistic value. With magnificent views of surrounding mountains, the village was, potentially, a major attraction for visitors."[2] The work of the Aga Khan Historic Cities Programme (AKHCP) consisted in the restoration of the mosques and public space using methods developed for Baltit Fort and Karimabad. The community pond (*pharee*) was rebuilt as were the towers and gates of the original fortifications. As has been the case elsewhere subsequent to AKHCP interventions, work on the public spaces of Ganish encouraged a number of house owners to follow suit. The thirty-three households of Ganish met in the restored *jataq* space in the spring of 2001 and created the Ganish Khun Heritage Social and Welfare Society to manage the conservation and rehabilitation of the village together with a number of social projects. Entrance tickets to the area generate income for the use of the community.

1 Masood Khan, in: Historic Cities Support Programme, 'Conservation and Development in Hunza and Baltistan'.
2 Ibid.

This page, the repaired community pond in Ganish, Pakistan, with restored enclosure walls and towers.

Right, the renovated *jataq* (community space) in Ganish, with a restored watchtower at the rear of the image.

Restoration of Shigar Fort Complex

BALTISTAN, NORTHERN AREAS, PAKISTAN

Architect/Planner:	Aga Khan Trust for Culture; Aga Khan Cultural Services (AKCS-P)
Funding Agency:	Aga Khan Trust for Culture; Government of Norway; Japanese Embassy (in Islamabad); Swiss Development Cooperation (SDC); Spanish, German, Greek and French Embassies (in Islamabad); Sumitomo Foundation; American Express International
Owner:	Aga Khan Trust for Culture
Date of Intervention:	1998
Completed:	2004

■ Set at an altitude of 2250 metres, Shigar Fort is located thirty kilometres from Skardu, the capital of Baltistan, on the Shigar River in the Northern Areas of Pakistan. Aga Khan Historic Cities Programme documentation explains: "The broader development project in Shigar includes restoration of mosques and rehabilitation of the settlements of Shilpa,

Left, view from the cliff behind the restored 17th-century Shigar Fort/Palace, Pakistan.

Right, the restored Khilingrong Mosque in the Shigar Fort complex.

Halpapa and Khilingrong, including upgrading of water and sanitation systems. The fourteenth-century Amburiq Mosque was restored to demonstrate that conservation of badly damaged monuments was feasible." The three structures of the Shigar Fort/Palace, today including a twenty-room guest house, are set on a thirty by nine metre stone platform. The original Shigar Fort Palace (known as Fong-Khar, which in the Balti language signifies "Palace on the Rock") was built by Hassan Khan, the twentieth ruler of the Amacha dynasty, in the early seventeenth century. Fong-Khar is the last remaining structure associated with the ruling Amacha family. Hassan Khan brought artisans from Kashmir to Shigar to build his palace. The result is a blend of Kashmiri-influenced carving and details with local Balti architecture. In 1999, Fong-Khar was given to the people of Baltistan by Raja Sahib Mohammad Ali Shah Saba of Shigar and the AKTC was entrusted with its restoration. In a painstaking six-year process, the entire site was brought back to life according to a strategy of adaptive reuse and restoration. This tri-partite strategy forms the concept behind work on the Shigar Fort Residence: preservation of cultural heritage; socially responsible tourism and economic development; and self-sustaining operations. A major goal of the Aga Khan Historic Cities Programme restoration was that the "project remain true to the original character and architecture of the buildings as much as possible." The project specifically encouraged the upgrading and rehabilitation of the village with micro-finance methods. As AKHCP documents describe the project: "The reuse concept for Shigar Fort Residence strikes a balance between, on the one hand, a museal site and, on the other, a very special resort-type guest house offering the unique experience of authentic guest rooms in a historic palace. The ongoing operations of Shigar Fort Residence strive toward long-term self-sustainability providing continuing economic and tourism development for the entire Shigar Valley."[1]

Since the AKTC remains the owner of the Shigar Fort/Palace, the organization ventures here into new territory, not only restoring buildings, but seeing to their ongoing use in a style that is respectful of the original monuments and of the need for the development of responsible tourism. The necessity of continued involvement in day-to-day operations of facilities like the Shigar Fort/Palace highlights the evolving nature of AKHCP programmes, where it has been clearly recognized that 'one-shot' interventions are rarely successful over the longer term.

1 See: http://www.shigarfort.com/aboutus.html#The%20Vision%20for%20Shigar%20Fort%20Residence.

Mostar Project Survey and Development Plans

MOSTAR, BOSNIA AND HERZEGOVINA

Architect/Planner:	Aga Khan Trust for Culture; World Monuments Fund
Funding Agency:	World Bank
Date of Intervention:	1998
Completed:	2001

■ Founded in the late fifteenth century, Mostar was the chief administrative city for the Ottoman Empire in the Herzegovina region. The Austro-Hungarian Empire absorbed Mostar in 1878 and it became part of the Kingdom of Yugoslavia after World War I, and in 1939 part of the Banovina of Croatia. Restoration of Mostar Old Town had received an Aga Khan Award in 1986 for work done by the agency Stari-Grad prior to the war, beginning in 1978. The city's symbol, called the Old Bridge or Stari Most, a twenty-nine-metre stone arch built high above the Neretva River in 1566 by the Ottoman architect Mimar Hajrudin, a student of Sinan, was destroyed (1993) like much of the Old City in the conflict of the early 1990s. A Pilot Cultural Heritage Project to restore the bridge and the Old City was launched in 1995 in a collaborative international assistance operation involving the World Bank, UNESCO, the Aga Khan Trust for Culture (AKTC) and the World Monuments Fund (WMF), in partnership with Bosnia and Herzegovina and the city of Mostar. The reconstruction of the bridge was completed in the spring of 2004 by a World Bank/UNESCO team. In parallel with this restoration of the Old Bridge, the AKTC and the WMF undertook a five-year restoration and rehabilitation effort in historic Mostar. As the Aga Khan Historic Cities Programme describes events: "To lay the ground for this comprehensive urban conservation effort, the AKTC/WMF team began in 1998 the preparation of a 'Conservation and Development Plan for the Old Town'. This Plan was formally adopted by the authorities on 15 May 2001. It includes plans, regulations and guidelines for the protection of the historic core of Mostar, detailed proposals for the rehabilitation of the neighbourhood areas, and a series of adaptive reuse schemes for priority buildings, as well as provisions to support institutional strengthening and active management of the historic city's future."[1] Recognizing the success of the combined efforts of the organizations involved, UNESCO formally included the historic centre of Mostar on its World Heritage List (2005, ref: 946rev). As the UNESCO inscription for Mostar reads: "The Old Bridge area, with its pre-Ottoman, eastern Ottoman, Mediterranean and western European architectural features, is an outstanding example of a multicultural urban settlement. The reconstructed Old Bridge and Old City of Mostar are a symbol of reconciliation, international cooperation and of the coexistence of diverse cultural, ethnic and religious communities. *Justification for Inscription*. Criterion vi. With the 'renaissance' of the Old Bridge and its surroundings, the symbolic power and meaning of the City of Mostar – as an exceptional and universal symbol of coexistence of communities from diverse cultural, ethnic and religious backgrounds – has been reinforced and strengthened, underlining the unlimited efforts of human solidarity for peace and powerful cooperation in the face of overwhelming catastrophes."[2]

1 See: http://www.akdn.org/news/mostar_230704.html.
2 See: http://whc.unesco.org/en/list/946.

View of the Biscevica and Lakisica complex in Mostar. In the background, the slim minaret of the reconstructed Neziraga Mosque.

Left, the restored Hindo Han with the minaret of the Neziraga Mosque to the rear.

Right, the Stari Most or Old Bridge of Mostar, not restored by the AKTC but by a World Bank/UNESCO team in 2004.

Below right, the entry side of the restored Muslibegovica house.

Conservation of Zanzibar Stone Town

ZANZIBAR, TANZANIA

Architect / Planner:	Aga Khan Trust for Culture; Aga Khan Cultural Services (AKCS-Z)
Funding Agency:	Aga Khan Trust for Culture; Aga Khan Fund for Economic Development; Tourism Promotion Services; European Union; UNCDF; UNCHS; UNDP; UNESCO; Governments of Finland, Germany and Italy
Owner:	Zanzibar Government; Waqf and Trust Commission
Date of Conservation Plans:	1992
Completed:	ongoing

■ Stone Town is the old section of Zanzibar City, the capital of the island of Zanzibar, Tanzania. Although Tanzania as a whole has a minority Muslim population (35%), Zanzibar is more than ninety-nine per cent Muslim. Stone buildings have been erected in the area since the 1830s, but the earliest settlements date back about 300 years. Extensive spice and slave trade with Asia and Africa passed through Zanzibar before Mombasa and Dar es Salaam took over these functions in the late nineteenth century. The influences generated through trade left their mark on local architecture that has Arab, Persian, Indian, Swahili and European elements. The Stone Town of Zanzibar became part of the UNESCO World Heritage list in 2000 (ref: 173rev). The organization's *Justification for Inscription* reads as follows:

Criterion II. The Stone Town of Zanzibar is an outstanding material manifestation of cultural fusion and harmonization.

Criterion III. For many centuries there was intense seaborne trading activity between Asia and Africa, and this is illustrated in an exceptional manner by the architecture and urban structure of the Stone Town.

Criterion VI. Zanzibar has great symbolic importance in the suppression of slavery, since it was one of the main slave-trading ports in East Africa and also the base from which its opponents such as David Livingstone conducted their campaign.[1]

The Aga Khan Historic Cities Programme (AKHCP) developed a strategic conservation plan with the Stone Town Conservation and Development Authority. A low-cost housing maintenance and repair programme was developed and a number of significant buildings on the waterfront were restored. This was the case of the Old Dispensary a dominant structure in the Port area that was inaugurated in 1997 as the Stone Town Cultural Centre. The Old Customs House was also restored. The former Telecom building, a deserted structure from the 1930s, was converted into a Serena Hotel by another Aga Khan organization, Tourism Promotion Services (TPS). Future plans are described by the AKHCP: "Landscaping plans have been drawn up and partly implemented to enhance the public areas around the string of historic and public buildings bordering the waterfront. In 2002–03, a comprehensive new development master plan for the complete waterfront was proposed, including a new passengers' terminal at the port, to be implemented with the government of Zanzibar and other donors. An Indian Ocean Maritime Museum is also being planned, adding to the town's cultural attractions and enhancing its public open spaces."

1 See: http://whc.unesco.org/en/list/173.

Before and after restoration images taken during the campaign of the Historic Cities Programme in Zanzibar, Tanzania.

Two panoramic views of the Stone Town
area of Zanzibar, Tanzania. The top image
shows a view over Omani Fort.

Stone Town Cultural Centre

ZANZIBAR, TANZANIA

Architect/Planner:	Aga Khan Trust for Culture; Aga Khan Cultural Services (AKCS-Z)
Date of Intervention:	1994
Completed:	1997

■ Converted in 1997 into the Stone Town Cultural Centre, this structure was built as the Tharia Topan Jubilee Hospital, with its foundation stone having been laid on 8 July 1887 to celebrate the fiftieth anniversary of the reign of Queen Victoria. Long used as a pharmacy and dispensary with a resident doctor, the structure was called the Old Dispensary. As Stephen Battle, the site architect, explains, the building was in poor condition when the AKTC took possession of it in 1991, due to thirty years of neglect and the difficult climate of Zanzibar. Stephen Battle writes: "The first stage of the conservation process involved the reconstruction of an idea of the original building through patient research and recording. A detailed assessment of the materials and construction methods was a critical part of the research process. The internal anatomy of the building was systematically examined in order to establish which materials were originally used and the methods and techniques by which they had been applied. This became the basis for an appropriate and effective conservation process."[1] Given its dominant location, the building was clearly the object of particular attention in its construction and decoration. Classical plaster mouldings designed by the architect Hashem Virjee Patel were carefully preserved or replaced where necessary. The woodwork of the building is another of its highlights. Battle writes: "The timber carving is unlike any other in the Stone Town in its sheer abundance and vivacity, and contrasts with the more restrained plaster work. Carved tendrils and stalks twist and curl through gables, flowers erupt from the brackets, and pineapples sprout from the ridges. Amidst the carved foliage, bright red, green, and blue panes of glass glitter like jewels. Eight massive columns, each one a single piece of timber forty centimetres square and over five metres long, support the principal beams running perpendicular and parallel to the facade." In methods typical of the Aga Khan Historic Cities Programme, trad-

itional craft skills were taught to local workers for this project, in the hope that their expertise would be usefully employed elsewhere in Zanzibar. Given that the interventions of the Aga Khan Trust for Culture in Zanzibar were numerous and remain a current priority for the organization, the influence of this exemplary restoration beyond the structure itself seems more than assured.

1 Stephen Battle, in: Historic Cities Support Programme, 'Zanzibar Stone Town Projects, Conservation Works in the Former Old Dispensary', to be found at: http://www.akdn.org/aktc/hcsp_zanzibar4.html.

Above right, the main facade of the restored Old Dispensary, now the Stone Town Cultural Centre, Zanzibar, Tanzania.

Left, the restored inner courtyard of the Old Dispensary, looking toward the main entrance. The building is notable because of its elaborate decorative plaster work and carvings (below right).

Zanzibar Serena Inn

ZANZIBAR, TANZANIA

Architect/Planner:	Aga Khan Trust for Culture; Aga Khan Cultural Services (AKCS-Z)
Date of intervention:	1994
Completed:	1997

■ One unusual aspect of the comprehensive involvement of the organizations of the Aga Khan in Zanzibar was that a hotel, the Zanzibar Serena Inn, was an integral part of the scheme. The former Telecommunications building, an abandoned 1930s structure in a prominent location on the seafront, was thus converted into a hotel with the same painstaking approach employed for the Old Dispensary. The Zanzibar Serena Inn is actually lodged in two historic seafront buildings that were joined together at the time of the restoration work. Next to the 1930s Telecommunications building, an eighteenth-century house was also integrated into the hotel. The hotel has fifty-one rooms and a swimming pool overlooking the ocean. Excursions into the Stone Town or to the Jozani Forest are organized by the hotel for its guests. The facility was inaugurated in 1997, at the same time as the restored Stone Town Cultural Centre. The Aga Khan Historic Cities Programme (AKHCP) declared: "Both projects constitute models for the wide range of interventions needed in the ongoing conservation and revitalization process of the Stone Town."

A branch of the Aga Khan Fund for Economic Development (AKFED) called Tourism Promotion Services (TPS) "seeks to develop tourism potential in selected areas in the developing world, particularly in under-served regions. It builds, rehabilitates and manages hotels and lodges that contribute to economic growth and the overall investment climate in an environmentally and culturally sensitive manner." Under the Serena name, AKFED owns and manages properties in Afghanistan, Kenya, Mozambique, Pakistan, Tajikistan, Tanzania and Uganda. The Serena hotels and lodges concerned place an emphasis on the training and hiring of local residents, and make extensive studies on their impact on the natural or urban environments into which they are to be inserted. Although Serena hotels and lodges are operated as profit-making enterprises, their presence and methods in a number of areas served by ongoing Aga Khan projects assure a source of revenue for those areas, an aspect of 'sustainable' restoration and development which is often overlooked by NGOs engaged in work similar to that of the AKHCP for example. Where the spice trade of another era left Zanzibar with a considerable architectural patrimony, the AKTC and related organizations have not only restored, but, in a broader sense, brought the Stone Town to life.

All fifty-one rooms of the Zanzibar Serena Inn look out onto the Indian Ocean.
The hotel is housed in two restored historic buildings, both on the seafront. As an integral part of the other historic preservation projects carried out by the AKHCP in Zanzibar, the Serena Inn offers a viable, durable way to develop and preserve the area.

Left, the restored
entrance to the upper
mosque and *madrasa*
of the Citadel of
Salah al-Din.

Right, an aerial view
of the Citadel of Salah
al-Din, Lattakia, Syria.

Citadel of Salah al-Din

LATTAKIA, SYRIA

Architect / Planner:	Aga Khan Trust for Culture; Syrian Directorate General of Antiquities and Museums (DGAM)
Funding Agency:	Aga Khan Trust for Culture; World Monuments Fund
Owner:	Syrian Ministry of Culture
Date of Intervention:	2000
Completed:	2006

■ The Citadel of Salah al-Din is located twenty-four kilometres east of Lattakia, Syria, in high mountainous terrain, on a ridge between two deep ravines, surrounded by forest. The castle was originally built in ancient times, possibly during the Phoenician period (early first millennium BC). The Phoenicians are said to have surrendered it to Alexander the Great about 334 BC. In the tenth century the Byzantines gained control of it, following which the castle was occupied by the Crusader Principality of Antioch. The Principality of Antioch, including parts of modern-day Turkey and Syria, was one of the states created during the First Crusade. Much of what remains visible today dates from the occupation of the Crusaders, which began around 1100. As the Aga Khan Historic Cities Programme report states: "They were responsible for constructing the

high stone walls and defensive towers, and cutting a deep moat into the rocks. In the middle of the moat rises a thin needle of remaining natural rock, twenty-eight-metres high, on which rested a bridge, once the only entry into the Citadel." The Crusader walls were breached by the armies of Salah al-Din in July 1188, and it is from this victory that the citadel takes its present name. Salah al-Din (Saladin, c. 1138–93) was a Kurdish Muslim general and warrior from Tikrit. He founded the Ayyubid dynasty of Egypt, Syria, Yemen (except for the Northern Mountains), Iraq, Mecca, Hejaz and Diyarbakir. Salah al-Din is an honorific title meaning "the Righteousness of the Faith" in Arabic. As it happens, the Ayyubid Wall restored by the AKHCP in Cairo (see page 102) was in part the work of Salah al-Din. The work of the Aga Khan Trust for Culture on the site began in 1999 with a detailed survey undertaken in cooperation with the Syrian authorities. The efforts of the AKHCP focused on the Palace complex, a part of the Citadel built beginning in 1188. This area is comprised of a mosque, a vaulted gallery, the Qala'un *hammam* and a palace complex with a *hammam*. One of a number of AKHCP projects in Syria, including work on the Citadel of Aleppo, the intervention on the Citadel of Salah al-Din was carried out using the tried and proven methods of the organization including the training of local professionals and craftsmen, investment in visitor infrastructure and the use of international standards of conservation practice and appropriate methodologies. The project at Salah al-Din will also include "the provision of a new visitors' centre and exhibition space in the restored mosque and *madrasa* buildings, and the AKTC will invest in other aspects of tourism infrastructure at the site such as toilet facilities, signage and pathways for visitors."

Humayun's Tomb Complex Gardens

DELHI, INDIA

Architect / Planner:	Aga Khan Trust for Culture
Funding Agency:	Aga Khan Trust for Culture; Archaeo-logical Survey of India (ASI); National Culture Fund; Indo-British Fiftieth Anniversary Trust; Oberoi Group of Hotels
Date of Intervention:	2000
Completed:	2003

■ The Tomb of the Mughal Emperor Humayun in Delhi was inscribed on the UNESCO World Heritage List in 1993 (ref: 232). Nasiruddin Humayun (1508–56) was the second Mughal Emperor and ruled northern parts of India from 1530 to 1540 and again from 1555 to 1556. The entry in the UNESCO list for his tomb states: "Built in 1570, [it] is of particular cultural significance as it was the first garden-tomb on the Indian subcontinent. It inspired several major architectural innovations, culminating in the construction of the Taj Mahal."[1] On the occasion of the fiftieth anniversary of India, the AKTC decided to sponsor the rehabilitation of Humayun's Garden. This was the first private restoration initiative involving a World Heritage Site in India. "The objective of the project," explains the Aga Khan Historic Cities Programme, "was to restore the gardens, pathways, fountains and water channels of the garden surrounding Humayun's Tomb according to the original plans of the builders. The preservation of historic elements required archival and archaeological research, as well as close attention to the living and renewable landscape elements. Site works encompassed a variety of disciplines, including archaeological excavation, the application of conservation science and hydraulic engineering. As part of the implementation process, a management plan was established to ensure proper long-term maintenance." Twelve hectares of lawn were planted, as well as 2500 trees in the course of the work. In his speech marking the inauguration of the gardens in 2003, the Aga Khan stated: "These restored gardens are the first *chahar-bagh*, or four-part paradise garden, to surround a Mughal tomb on the sub-continent. Built nearly a century before the Taj Mahal, the Tomb and its gardens were an expression of

the love and respect borne toward the Emperor Humayun by his son, Akbar, and widow, Haji Begum. The *chahar-bagh* was more than a pleasure garden. In the discipline and order of its landscaped geometry, its octagonal or rectangular pools, its selection of favourite plants and trees, it was an attempt to create transcendent perfection – a glimpse of paradise on earth." More than a simple restoration, the work undertaken at Humayun's Tomb can be seen as emblematic of the initiatives of the Aga Khan Historic Cities Programme – initiatives described by the Aga Khan himself in Dehli: "Speaking of civil society, central to my broader concern is the fact that investing in such cultural initiatives represents an opportunity to improve the quality of life for the people who live around these remarkable inheritances of past great civilizations. The Aga Khan Trust for Culture insists that each of its conservation and restoration projects should be able to have an important positive impact on that quality of life. We are keen that our investments create a multiplier effect in the local economy. Accordingly, we monitor their impact on the physical environment as well as on disposable income and other indices of better living conditions. We also emphasize self-sustainability … These restored gardens can thus become the fulcrum and catalyst for socio-economic development as well as an irreplaceable resource for education."[2]

1 See: http://whc.unesco.org/pg.cfm?cid=31&id_site=232.
2 Speech by His Highness the Aga Khan at the ceremony to inaugurate the restored Humayun's Tomb Gardens, New Delhi, India, 15 April 2003.

The Emperor Humayun was the son of Babur, founder of the Mughal Empire. His tomb was built over a period of about a decade beginning in 1565 and contains over a hundred Mughal graves. It stands on a 120-square-metre platform in New Delhi, India.

Restoration of the Great Mosque

MOPTI, MALI

Architect / Planner: Aga Khan Trust for Culture

Funding Agency: Aga Khan Trust for Culture

Date of Intervention: 2004

Completed: 2006

■ Mopti is the fourth largest city in Mali with a population of 118,000. It is located at the confluence of the Niger and Bani Rivers, between Timbuktu and Ségou, about a hundred kilometres from the border of Burkina Faso. It is the landlocked country's most important port but was founded only in the nineteenth century. The population of Mali is ninety per cent Muslim. The Grand Mosque of Mopti is an earthen structure built in the traditional Sudanese style between 1936 and 1943 on the site of an earlier mosque built in 1903. The first phase of AKTC work involved the repair of the roof and the stabilization of the upper part of the building. A poor restoration carried out with cement in 1978 had weakened the structure. On 14 October 2004, the monument was formally inscribed as an official landmark in the nation's cultural heritage by the Minister for Culture. Beginning in November 2004 local masons working under AKHCP supervision removed the cement and replaced it with traditional mortar and bricks in strict observance of traditional construction techniques. The work was carried out under the supervision of the Direction Nationale du Patrimoine du Ministère de la Culture du Mali, regional authorities, the city of Mopti and the Mosque's committee. During a visit in the course of restoration in 2005, the Aga Khan declared: "Mopti's mosque is an outstanding example of the traditional Muslim architecture of the Sahel. We hope that our restoration efforts, which include an important training component, will develop appropriate restoration guidelines and solutions that will be used in other projects in Mali and in the region."[1] As a result of the project, certificates were awarded to two master builders, seventeen bricklayers, eighteen skilled labourers, five carpenters and eleven craft workers amongst other professionals. On 19 June 2006, the Aga Khan Development Network (AKDN) formally handed over the keys of the Great Mosque of Mopti to the Malian Minis-

ter of Culture, who in turn gave them to Kissima Touré, head of the village of Mopti. Like the Great Mosque in Niono, Mali, which received the Aga Khan Award for Architecture (1983 Cycle), this structure calls on techniques and architectural forms that clearly have their roots in periods that date from before the actual twentieth-century construction. The efforts of the organizations of the Aga Khan give value to what must be termed local traditions that have surely been undervalued by Western specialists of architectural history. With similar efforts undertaken in Djenné, or Timbuktu, the AKTC has shown its commitment to ongoing efforts concentrated in specific regions selected because of the importance of local architectural patrimony. On the occasion of the visit to Mopti of the Aga Khan in 2005, Amadou Toumani Touré, President of the Republic of Mali, declared: "On behalf of the people of Mali and the government, I would like to say we are honoured that the AKDN is contributing to the preservation of the country's cultural heritage."[2] This statement underlines the fully collaborative nature of the interventions of organizations like the Aga Khan Historic Cities Programme, spearheaded by the Aga Khan himself.

1 See: http://www.akdn.org/news/2005Aug01.htm.
2 Ibid.

Restoration work on the Great Mosque in Mopti, Mali, was carried out between November 2004 and June 2006 and was conducted in strict observance of traditional construction techniques. Further initiatives of this kind are notably in Djenné and Timbuktu.

View of the restoration work.
Mopti is set on three islands
linked by dykes: the New Town,
the Old Town and Bani.

A facade of the mosque and ongoing restoration work. Djingareyber, or the Great Mosque, is Timbuktu's oldest monument and its major landmark. Located at the western corner of the old town, the mosque is almost entirely built in raw earth which is used for mud bricks and rendering.

Restoration of Djingareyber Mosque

TIMBUKTU, MALI

Architect/Planner:	Aga Khan Trust for Culture
Funding Agency:	Aga Khan Trust for Culture
Date of intervention:	2006
Planned completion:	2010

■ One of the most recent restoration projects undertaken by the Aga Khan Historic Cities Programme (AKHCP) concerns the Djingareyber Mosque, one of the three great mosques (with Sankore and Sidi Yahia) of Timbuktu. The city of Timbuktu is located in Mali, about fifteen kilometres north of the northernmost loop of the Niger River. It was established by Tuareg nomads as a seasonal camp in about AD 1100. At its height, Timbuktu was at the crossroads of three major trading routes between West Africa and Tripoli, Alexandria and Cairo to the northeast. As early as the fourteenth century, significant books were written and copied in Timbuktu, establishing the city as a centre of written tradition in Africa. By the time of the reign of the Askias (1494–1591) Timbuktu had become an important centre of Koranic studies with the University of Sankore and as many as 180 *madrasas* with 25,000 students from numerous Muslim countries.

Built in 1325 or 1327, the Djingareyber Mosque was designed by Abu Isahp Es-Saheli, who was paid 200 kilos of gold for his efforts by Kankan Moussa, Emperor of the Mali Empire. Francesco Siravo of the AKTC explains: "All of the walls of the mosque are made of local limestone, called *alhore* bound with earthen mortar and covered with plaster (*banco*). In this respect, Timbuktu's construction materials differ from those of Mopti and Djenné where walls are constructed with earthen brick. The mosque was entirely rebuilt between 1570 and 1583 by the Imam al-Aqib, Cadi of Timbuktu, who enlarged the structure and created the exterior wall around the courtyard and the cemetery to the west."[1] It has three inner courts and two minarets, a pyramidal central one and another conical one along the seventy-metre-long eastern facade. The mosque has prayer space for approximately 2000 people.

The region of Timbuktu, including such monuments as Djingareyber Mosque, was added to the UN-ESCO World Heritage list in 1988 (ref:119rev). The description associated with this listing explains that as the "home of the prestigious Koranic Sankore University and other *madrasas*, Timbuktu was an intellectual and spiritual capital and a centre for the propagation of Islam throughout Africa in the fifteenth and sixteenth centuries. Its three great mosques, Djingareyber, Sankore and Sidi Yahia, recall Timbuktu's golden age. Although continuously restored, these monuments are today under threat from desertification."[2] In 1989, the building was included in the list of World Heritage sites in danger and five years later the World Heritage Committee responded favourably to the local Cultural Mission's request for assistance. Funds were provided for training and emergency interventions carried out by a team from CRATerre-EAG. In 2000, the building was removed from the list of World Heritage sites in danger.

Although voyagers commented about the degraded state of some walls of the mosque as early as the 1830s, the structure has been continually shored up or resurfaced in a local practice involving the participation of the faithful. Analysis carried out by the AKHCP revealed problems associated with the quality of construction materials used in relatively recent times, with the evacuation of water, and with the presence of animals within the mosque. The southern facade, in particular, shows substantial signs of erosion by water and wind. Plans for the restoration of the mosque imply the respect of the existing context including alterations made subsequent to construction, the need to conserve or restore elements rather than replacing them, and the return to the use of the higher quality materials which analysis of the building shows were used in earlier times. As in the case of other AKHCP projects, the programme will identify and make use of local skilled labourers and train others. Work on the environment of the mosque, its walls and foundations, the reconstruction of the roof and drainage system, and intervention on the interior and exterior wall coatings is planned over a series of four yearly campaigns to be completed in 2010.

1 E-mail from Francesco Siravo, 29 January 2007.
2 See: http://whc.unesco.org/en/list/119.

Old City of Kabul

KABUL, AFGHANISTAN

Architect/Planner:	Aga Khan Trust for Culture; Department of Historic Monuments; Institute of Archaeology of the Ministry of Information and Culture
Funding Agency:	Aga Khan Trust for Culture: German Government
Date of Intervention:	2000
Completed:	ongoing

■ The city of Kabul has been in the news frequently in recent years because of conflicts. It might be said that war and conquest is inscribed in its history. Founded over 3000 years ago, Kabul became the capital of the Mughal Empire in 1504, under the rule of Zahir al-Din Mohammad (Babur, 1483–1530). Timur Shah Durrani, Shah of Afghanistan from 1776 to his death in 1793, made it the capital of what would become modern Afghanistan. Long before these events, in 674, the Islamic invasions conquered Kabul, and then it was successively ruled by the Samanids, the Hindu Shahi dynasty, the Ghaznavids, Ghorids and Timurids, before the arrival of the Mughals and the Durranis. In part because of this history, Kabul is today a multicultural and multi-ethnic city. The engagement of the Aga Khan in the restoration of the Old City of Kabul in 2000 was an early and significant step toward the rehabilitation programme of the country. After the end of the war, an agreement was concluded between the Interim Administration and the AKTC "to restore, rehabilitate and upgrade a number of significant historic buildings and public open spaces in the city. The first building selected was the Timur Shah Mausoleum, in the heart of the bazaar district." The dome was restored in 2004, with the consolidation of the rest of the building and the enhancement of "the former public garden in front of it by providing alternative premises for the squatting tradesmen" as the subsequent goals of the AKTC team lead by Jolyon Leslie. The site of AKTC intervention is the Bagh-i Babur (Babur Gardens), originally laid out by the founder of the Mughal dynasty. The Bagh-i Babur is a terraced and walled open space containing the tomb of the sixteenth-century emperor, and features the remains of what was the first Mughal 'paradise garden' and the predecessor of many famous imperial gardens in the South Asian sub-continent. As presented by the Aga Khan Historic Cities Programme (AKHCP): "This garden is one of the most important public open spaces of Kabul and its rehabilitation will not only re-establish the historic character of the site with its water channels, planted terraces and pavilions, but also provide a much appreciated space for leisure, meetings, celebrations, open-air receptions and cultural events." The organizations are also working in the Asheqan-i Arefan neighbourhood to aid with the repair of historic houses and the restoration of monuments such as the Uzbeka Mosque. Given the unsettled political situation in Afghanistan, the early and continued aid efforts of the Aga Khan Trust for Culture, through its HCP branch, demonstrate the commitment of the Aga Khan to the culture and architecture of Muslim cities. The depth of this effort is indicated by other indicatives such as the participation of the Aga Khan Fund for Economic Development (AKFED) in the creation of Afghanistan's GSM telecommunications system, the creation of a training programme for nurses by the Aga Khan University (Karachi), which counted eighty-nine graduates in 2006, and the participation of the Aga Khan Development Network in the management and supervision of the French Medical Institute for Children in Kabul.

The restored Mausoleum of Timur Shah Durrani, Shah of Afghanistan (from 1776 to 1793), who made Kabul the capital of Afghanistan.

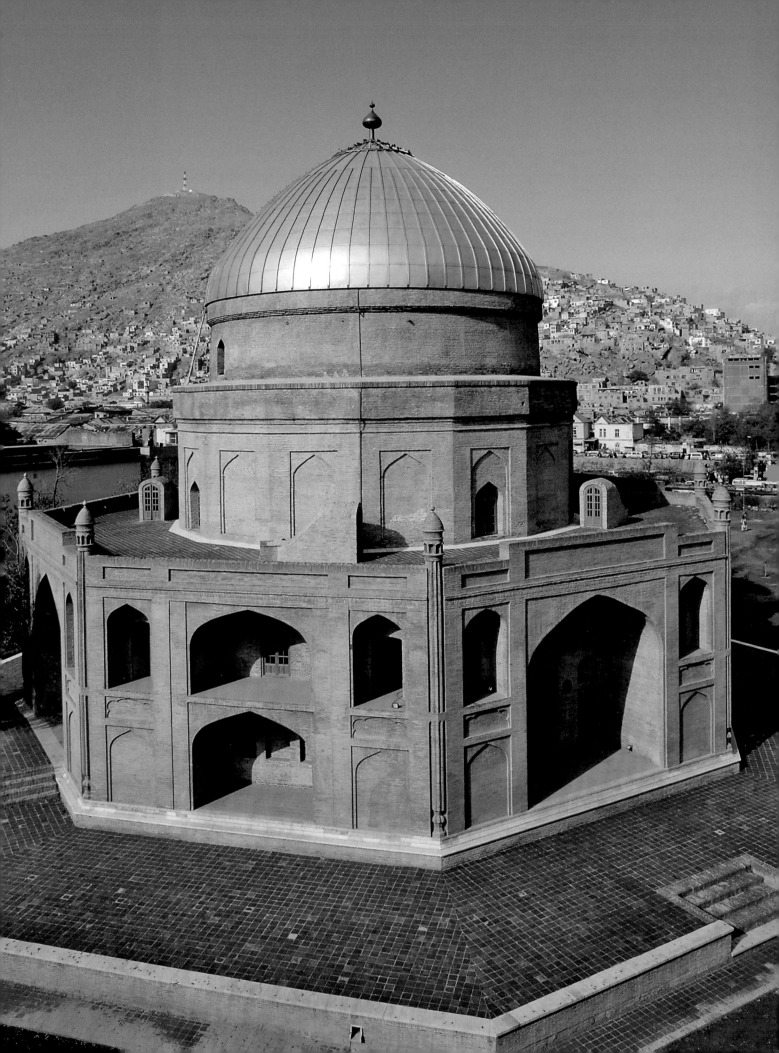

Two images of pavement and drain works (after restoration, top) in the Old City of Kabul near the Babur Gardens.

The Baghi-i Babur (Babur Gardens) in Kabul, Afghanistan, before and after restoration work undertaken by the AKHCP.

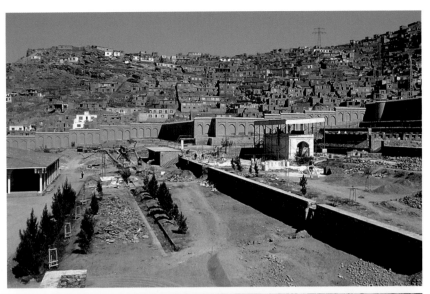

Kabul Serena Hotel

KABUL, AFGHANISTAN

Architect:	Ramesh Khosla
Funding Agency:	Aga Khan Fund for Economic Development (AKFED)
Owner:	Tourism Promotion Services (TPS)
Date of Intervention:	2002
Completed:	2005

■ The Kabul Serena Hotel is located in the centre of the city overlooking Zarnegar Park.

Built in 1945, amid landscaped gardens, the former Kabul Hotel, destroyed during the war, underwent a complete refurbishment, through the rehabilitation of the existing building and the addition of a completely new section. The phased upgrading of the original structure at a cost of USD 35 million, has yielded 177 guest rooms, two restaurants and a shopping arcade. A spokesman for the Aga Khan Foundation for Economic Development, Aly Mawji, was quoted by *Time Magazine* as saying: "Mainstream tourism is still years away, but we hope the hotel will encourage some more adventurous travellers." Explaining this intervention and indeed the overall presence of his organizations in the country, the Aga Khan asked an obvious, but still surprising, question: "Ladies and gentlemen, there are some who will ask: why build a hotel in Afghanistan at this stage of its struggle for development? And why build one of a five star level?" His explanation has to do with local circumstances, but also with the concept of collaboration with local authorities that has governed AKTC action around the Muslim world: "In 2002, the government of Afghanistan asked the Aga Khan Development Network – the AKDN – to help in restoring Kabul's hotel capacity, which had been almost totally destroyed by the civil war … The government wanted to ensure that state visitors, diplomats, government officials, foreign and local investors, donor agency representatives and tourists travelling to Kabul would have acceptable accommodation. The Kabul Hotel had been a notable landmark and centre of activity in the city since it was built in 1945; hence it was an obvious candidate for restoration." Finally, how does the Kabul Serena Hotel fit into the overall scheme of intervention by other AKDN organizations? In the words of

the Aga Khan: "As a significant development asset, the Kabul Serena Hotel is a major commitment within the broader mission of the Aga Khan Development Network's nine development agencies which work in concert on the many facets of human development. Regardless of gender, origin or faith, the Aga Khan Development Network strives to help the weakest in society to achieve self-reliance in improving their lives, guided by the Koranic ethic of a common humanity and the dignity of all mankind. Aga Khan Development Network affiliate agencies began that mission in Afghanistan in 1995 with refugee resettlement and emergency humanitarian assistance. Since 2001, our agencies have been engaged in longer term development across the full spectrum of human need: economic, social and cultural."[1]

1 Speech by His Highness the Aga Khan at the opening of the Kabul Serena Hotel, Afghanistan, 8 November 2005.

The creation of the Kabul Serena Hotel is part of a coherent series of projects launched by the agencies of the Aga Khan in the immediate wake of the end of hostilities in 2002. The work of the Historic Cities Programme is thus just one part of this multi-tiered intervention.

THE AGA KHAN
PROGRAM
FOR ISLAMIC
ARCHITECTURE

The Aga Khan Program for Islamic Architecture

I have selected two of America's most distinguished architectural schools – Harvard and MIT – and established a programme for Islamic architecture. This programme will not only utilize their immense intellectual resources for the benefit of scholars seeking to understand Islamic architecture, but also circulate this expertise among students, teachers and universities in Muslim and Western countries.[1]

His Highness the Aga Khan

Established in 1979, the Aga Khan Program for Islamic Architecture (AKPIA) at Harvard University and the Massachusetts Institute of Technology (MIT) is supported by endowments from the Aga Khan that "support instruction, research and student aid … the Aga Khan Program for Islamic Architecture is dedicated to the study of Islamic architecture, urbanism, visual culture and conservation in an effort to respond to the cultural and educational needs of a diverse constituency drawn from all over the world. Along with the focus on improving the teaching of Islamic art and architecture and setting excellence as the standard in professional research, the Aga Khan Program for Islamic Architecture also continually strives to promote the visibility of pan-Islamic cultural heritage." The Aga Khan Program for Islamic Architecture was the fruit of conversations between the Aga Khan and the Presidents of Harvard and MIT that took place in the late 1970s. With the encouragement and participation of Professors Oleg Grabar (Harvard), William Porter (MIT) and others, AKPIA took the form of endowed professorships at the two institutions with supporting publications, such as the journal of Islamic studies *Muqarnas*. The creation of AKPIA coincided within two years with that of the Aga Khan Award for Architecture. As the Aga Khan himself underlines, the Award was not conceived in the specific goal of teaching, so an educational component to his commitment to architecture in the Islamic world was necessary. The question arose of whether to seek to endow institutions in the Muslim world or rather to select Western universities. Perhaps in part because he was educated at Harvard, but also for other carefully thought-out reasons, the Aga Khan decided that Harvard and MIT would be at the heart of this Program. The two institutions, both located in Cambridge, Massachusetts, have a long history of fruitful collaboration, but also a number of significant differences in their curricula and traditions. The influence of the Aga Khan Program for Islamic Architecture on the study of Islamic art and architecture in the United States has been undeniable – with a large number of graduates from the Program teaching across the country, often in newly created positions that might not have existed had AKPIA not been created. AKPIA graduates are also a significant factor in a number of universities in the Muslim world. With the selection of professors born in Muslim countries today (Gülru Necipoglu, Turkey; Nasser Rabbat, Syria; and Hashim Sarkis, Lebanon), the Aga Khan Program for Islamic Architecture has also contributed to a shift away from what might be termed the 'Orientalist' approach to the study of Islamic art and architecture to one that has sought out and discovered many of the roots of the originality and creativity of countries sometimes underestimated in the West.

As is usually the case, the Aga Khan's own explanation of the reasons for creating the Aga Khan Program for Islamic Architecture is the clearest and most convincing of arguments: "As a student of history, you learn about the cultural processes of history. I was looking at the physical environment in the developing world, and I had to ask myself what we were doing correctly, or incorrectly. My sense was that while there was a fairly good understanding of programmatic requirements, the contextualization of those programmatic requirements in our part of the world just did not exist. Conceptualizing the Program began in the mid 1970s. Those involved in the process came at it with a sense of humility in the face of issues that were sensed, but that had never been intellectualized or rationalized. We started with an enormous process of inquiry. The industrialized world was dominating the processes of change in the Third World, and that domination resulted in an educational process in the Islamic world that was First-World driven. Therefore, we had to accept that an educational role was necessary. The question was how to design an educational resource that would have the maximum possible impact and, at the same time, have a legitimacy which would make it acceptable to much of the Islamic world. That became the basis for the Aga Khan Program for Islamic Architecture at Harvard University and the Massachusetts Institute of Technology."[2]

1 His Highness the Aga Khan, quoted in http://www.akdn.org/aktc/AKPIA_BR.pdf.
2 His Highness the Aga Khan, quoted in psb 03-02-0140 Aga Khan Development Network http://akdn.org.

ArchNet.org

The Aga Khan has always taken an interest in the dissemination of information and knowledge concerning the programmes he funds. More specifically, he has sought to "find ways in which the profound humanistic tradition of Islam could inform the concept and construction of buildings and public spaces." The architecture magazine *Mimar* and the Islamic arts journal *Muqarnas* have been indications of this continuing preoccupation. The Aga Khan held a series of meetings in 1998 with the President of MIT, Charles Vest, and the Dean of MIT's School of Architecture and Planning, William Mitchell, with the goal of enlarging the scope of the Program he created at Harvard and MIT in 1977, the Aga Khan Program for Islamic Architecture (AKPIA). The result of these talks was the creation of ArchNet (http://archnet.org), a website, or perhaps more correctly an online community that aims to provide information on architecture, planning and landscape design in the developing world with a focus on Muslim cultures, and to allow students, teachers or practitioners to contact people with similar interests all over the world. Originally developed in collaboration with the MIT Press, ArchNet is funded by the AKTC and developed and administered at MIT's School of Architecture and Planning with the co-operation of the School of Architecture at the University of Texas, Austin. At the heart of ArchNet is a digital library that draws upon the resources of the AKTC archives, the Documentation Centre of the Aga Khan Program for Islamic Architecture at Harvard University and the Rotch Visual Collections at MIT. This vast repository of images, project files and publications is free of charge to users. Most of the files concerning the Aga Khan Award for Architecture, including field reports, project portfolios and seminar and Award publications, are readily available on the site. As Charles Vest stated on 27 September 2002 at the official launching of the site: "ArchNet fulfils the original promise of the Internet, it provides accessibility to teaching resources that are currently unavailable to many universities, while creating a worldwide online community that is constantly enriching the contents of the catalogue. Everyone benefits. At MIT, we benefit from the upload of unique resources from ArchNet partner schools, while schools around the world have the opportunity to choose teaching materials from the combined resources of MIT, Harvard, the Aga Khan Trust for Culture and other partner schools."[1] Given that many potential users of this network do not have ready access to substantial architecture libraries or other source material, ArchNet can indeed claim to be the largest and richest initiative of its kind in terms of content and global reach. Shiraz Allibhai, the former director of ArchNet, now working with the AKTC in Geneva, cites up-to-date figures for the site: "As of February 2007, ArchNet had over 39,000 members from 173 countries. The holdings of its Digital Library have increased to over 52,000 images and 4000 files, illustrating more than 5000 historic and contemporary buildings and urban projects in ninety-five countries around the world. It supports an impres-

Promotional material for the ArchNet.org website explains its overall goals in a few words.

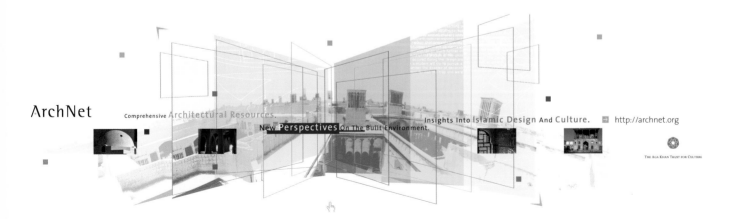

ArchNet   Comprehensive Architectural Resources.
                 New Perspectives On The Built Environment.   Insights Into Islamic Design And Culture.   http://archnet.org

THE AGA KHAN TRUST FOR CULTURE

ArchNet

ArchNet seeks to enable participants to learn how to enhance the quality of the built environment in their communities; to compensate for a lack of resources at their academic institutions; to honor the rich legacy of their cultures; and to celebrate the humanistic traditions of Islam.

"It is my hope that ArchNet will become a global resource that serves people who are working for positive change in the physical environment within Islamic societies."

His Highness the Aga Khan

BUILDING A GLOBAL COMMUNITY

sive average of some 8600 unique users on a daily basis who download 37Gb of information in the form of images, publications and files on a weekly basis. In 2006, over 493,000 publications and project files, with a focus on the built environment of the Muslim world that would otherwise have been unavailable, were downloaded by ArchNet users." Allibhai goes on to say that William Mitchell, now Professor of Architecture and Media Arts and Sciences, MIT, is currently supervising an update of the site (ArchNet v2.0) taking into account "an Open Source and Open Content framework that will provide long-term sustainability. ArchNet v2.0 will take much greater advantage of the energy and creativity of the user community, which will be less one of passive content consumers and more one of active content creators."

1 See: http://www.akdn.org/news/archnet_270902.html.

Stari Most (Old Bridge), Mostar, Bosnia-
Herzegovina. Photograph (albumen print)
by an unidentified Austrian photographer,
c. 1890. Courtesy of the Fine Arts Library,
Harvard College Library.

Collections Documenting the Middle East at Harvard's Fine Arts Library

The establishment in 1979 of the Aga Khan Program for Islamic Architecture (AKPIA) included the creation of a Documentation Centre at the Fine Arts Library of Harvard University. The funding involved came with a mandate to increase the Library's holdings of publications and photographic images documenting Islamic visual culture. Harvard has the oldest academic library in North America and one of the largest in the world. It has been acquiring books about the arts and architecture of the Muslim world for more than two centuries. The University's Fogg Art Museum, established in 1891, collected Islamic art almost from the start, but it was the Aga Khan's endowment of a Documentation Centre that has made it possible to create a research resource that is unparalleled in the depth of its documentation and in the facilities and specialized staff assistance it offers. Among the books and visual materials acquired for the Library with Aga Khan Program funds are many that are extremely rare or unique. While the main goal of the AKPIA Documentation Centre is to support teaching and research on the history of art and architecture, it also serves as a resource to record and help preserve a past that is in danger of disappearing due to development, natural disasters or conflict.

The earliest systematic acquisitions at Harvard of photographs of the Middle East were made by Professor David Gordon Lyon, starting in 1891 in his first year as curator at Harvard's Semitic Museum, founded two years before with the primary goal of providing "a thorough study and a better knowledge of Semitic history and civilization, so that the world shall better understand and acknowledge the debt it owes to the Semitic people," according to its founding document. As Jeff Spurr, Islamic and Middle East Specialist with the Aga Khan Program for Islamic Architecture in the Fine Arts Library at Harvard University explains, the collections "now present at the Fine Arts Library are essentially of two species, following two very different models of organization, the first, that of an archive, the second, that of a visual library devoted to art historical documentation. The first comprises about 80,000 historical photographs of the Middle East and adjacent regions, which include Afghanistan, Central Asia, Islamic South Asia, the Balkans, the Caucasus, Sudan and Islamic Spain. In the core regions –

Egypt, the Maghreb, Palestine, Lebanon, Syria, Arabia, Turkey, Iraq and Iran – this collecting was undertaken irrespective of subject, covering ancient, Biblical, classical, Islamic, ethnographic, landscape and tourist subjects, limited only by what nineteenth- and early twentieth-century photographers deemed worthy of photographing, although extending in a couple of instances to the 1950s and 1960s. The second comprises upwards of 180,000 photographs and slides documenting the whole of Islamic visual culture." As circumstances would have it, Oleg Grabar came to Harvard as Professor of Islamic Art in 1969. He brought a desire to expand both photograph and slide collections in the Fine Arts Library, which was "a new institution, resulting from the merger of the Fogg Art Museum and Widener Library collections in 1963, physically located in the Fogg, but institutionally a part of the Harvard College Library," according to Jeff Spurr. Professor Grabar is one of the central figures who assisted the Aga Khan in the creation of both the Award and the AKPIA. Professor Grabar served on the Steering Committee of the Award in the first three cycles, and was a member of the Master Jury in the 1989 Cycle. The fact that the Fine Arts Library was endowed from the outset as part of the AKPIA Program is surely a testimony to the influence of Oleg Grabar. Given the long history and already rich collections of the Library, dating back more than 200 years, the impetus given through the funding provided by the Aga Khan, together with the very professional work of those responsible for the conservation and acquisition of books and images, the resources at Harvard are surely amongst the most complete in the world. By encouraging the collection of images such as those conserved at Harvard, the Aga Khan clearly aims to allow scholars and others to see the world that went before them so that they may better understand the present and the future.

The Aga Khan Professors

The success of the Aga Khan Program for Islamic Architecture (AKPIA) at Harvard and MIT is undoubtedly in good part connected with the professors affiliated with the Program.[1] The variety of their experience is a clear indication of the ambitions of AKPIA. Oleg Grabar was the first Aga Khan Professor of Islamic Art and Architecture when that chair was established at Harvard in 1980. Ronald Lewcock, an architect, conservator and scholar, was Aga Khan Professor of Architecture at MIT (1984–91). There are currently three Aga Khan Professors at Harvard and MIT.

Gülru Necipoglu is in fact a product of AKPIA since she was one of the Program's first graduate students, receiving her Ph.D. from Harvard in 1986. A member of the Harvard faculty beginning from the following year, she was named Aga Khan Professor of Islamic Art at Harvard in 1993. Born in Turkey, she is a specialist of Ottoman art and architecture. Her books include *Architectural Culture in the Age of Sinan: Memory, Identity and Decorum* (Reaktion Books, 2004); *The Topkapi Scroll: Geometry and Ornament in Islamic Architecture* (Getty Centre, 1995, which won the Albert Hourani Book Award and the Spiro Kostoff Book Award for Architecture and Urbanism); and *Architecture, Ceremony and Power: The Topkapi Palace in the Fifteenth and Sixteenth Centuries* (MIT Press, 1991). She is convinced that AKPIA has played a significant role in scholarship in her area. As she says: "Taken as a whole, the Program has helped elevate the study of Islamic art and architecture from a relatively marginal position in Western academia, and exposes both students and the global architectural community to the many facets and dimensions of this burgeoning field. I believe that the Islamic tradition is analogous to the American notion of the 'melting pot,' in which a pluralistic blending of cultures, traditions and aesthetics has resulted in a rich mosaic. There is a need – and a demand – for specialists who are qualified to explore and enrich the cross-cultural threads of this complex tapestry. The Aga Khan Program for Islamic Architecture is one of the few places where students can experience the breadth of Islamic art and architecture in an environment that offers virtually unlimited academic and intellectual resources."[2]

Nasser Rabbat, born in Syria, is the Aga Khan Professor of Islamic Architecture at MIT, where he has been teaching since 1991. Before joining the faculty in 1991, Rabbat worked as a designer in Los Angeles and in Damascus. His broad interests range from Mamluk architecture, or the transition between late antique and early Islamic architecture in Syria, to contemporary architecture in the Islamic world. His books include *The Citadel of Cairo: A New Interpretation of Royal Mamluk Architecture* (E. J. Brill, 1995), and *Thaqafat al Bina' wa Bina' al-Thaqafa* [The Culture of Building and Building Culture] (Riad Alrayyes Publisher, 2002). He contributes regularly to journals in Arabic including: *Wughat Nazar*, *Akhbar al-Adab*, *Jaridat al-Funun*, *al-Hayat* and *al-Mustaqbal*. "The most profound achievement of the Aga Khan Program for Islamic Architecture, in my opinion," he says, "is to argue for a critical reappraisal of the dominant paradigm of architectural history, which legitimizes a self-conscious and evolving Western architectural tradition while casting the architecture of other cultures in changeless 'types.'" An interesting aspect of Professor Rabbat's position is that he feels there is a direct relationship between historical issues of interest and the current situation. He says of AKPIA: "The Program focuses on three critical issues at the core of architectural education in an effort to respond to the cultural and pedagogical needs of a diverse Islamic world. First is the question of the universality of architectural education in an age of rapid change, both in the conception and transfer of knowledge and in the definition of academic fields. Second is the nature of architecture in view of the proliferation of new theoretical models and technological devices that are reconfiguring both the discipline and the practice of architecture. Third is the agency of culture in shaping forms and meanings, especially in the Islamic and developing worlds, where architecture can still play a powerful social and environmental role."[3] The third and most recently named (2002) of the AKPIA professors is Hashim Sarkis, the first Aga Khan Professor of Landscape Architecture and Urbanism in Muslim Societies at the Harvard Graduate School of Design. Born in Lebanon, in 1964, he was Harvard's director of Masters and Doctorate of Design Studies Programs (2002–05).

He studied at the Rhode Island School of Design and at Harvard. He has worked as a practising architect in the Lebanon and in the United States and has published various books including the CASE publication series (GSD/Prestel) and *Circa 1958: Lebanon in the Pictures and Plans of Constantinos Doxiadis* (Dar An-Nahar Publishers, Beirut, 2003). Prior to creating his own firm, Hashim Sarkis Architecture Landscape Urban Design in Cambridge, Massachusetts, in 1998, Hashim Sarkis worked with Rafael Moneo on a project for the souks of Beirut, and was Programmes Director of Plan B, a non-profit organization "involved in improving the quality of the built environment in Lebanon and the Middle East." His academic research projects at Harvard include 'New Geographies' and 'Urbanization in Turkey', a study of the changing patterns of urbanization in Turkey and the relationship between rural and urban development.

1 See: http://web.mit.edu/akpia/www/.
2 Quoted in psb 03-02-0140 Aga Khan Development Network http://akdn.org.
3 Ibid.

Qal'at Sim'an, built around the column of Simeon Stylites, Syria; octagon, interior, great apse, photograph *c.* 1920s. Collection of Professor A. Kingsley Porter (no photographer credited), Courtesy of the Fine Arts Library, Harvard College Library. Image selected by Professor Nasser Rabbat, who explains: "My research focuses on the overlapping intercultural spaces where peoples have always met and exchanged ideas, views, beliefs and practices, and, in the process, created architecture."

THE PRIORITY
OF EDUCATION

The Priority of Education

At the height of the Islamic civilization, Muslim academies of higher learning reached from Spain to India and from North Africa to Afghanistan. Muslim scholars reached pinnacles of achievement in astronomy, geography, physics, philosophy, mathematics and medicine. It is no exaggeration to say that the original Christian universities of the Latin West, at Paris, Bologna and Oxford, indeed the whole European Renaissance, received a vial influx of new knowledge from the Islamic world: an influx from which later Western colleges and universities were to benefit in turn, including those of North America.[1]

His Highness the Aga Khan

It is apparent from the emphasis placed by the Aga Khan on education in various forms that he views this as one of his most significant priorities. He states clearly that he is inspired by the educational traditions of Islam. More recently, his own grandfather, Sir Sultan Mohamed Shah, Aga Khan III, oversaw the creation of 200 schools in the first half of the twentieth century, the first of them in 1905 in Zanzibar, Gwadur, Pakistan and Mundra, India. The Aga Khan Education Services (AKES), an outgrowth of these early initiatives, currently operates more than 300 schools and advanced educational programmes that provide quality pre-school, primary, secondary and higher secondary education services to students in Pakistan, India, Bangladesh, Kenya, Uganda, Tanzania and Tajikistan. In 2000, the Aga Khan launched a new initiative for education from "pre-primary through higher secondary" education in the form of the Aga Khan Academies. The first of these opened in Mombasa, Kenya, in 2003, and thirteen similar institutions are currently in various stages of planning in Tanzania, India, the Democratic Republic of the Congo, Madagascar, Mali, Mozambique, Uganda, Bangladesh, Pakistan, Afghanistan, the Kyrgyz Republic, Tajikistan and Syria. Another branch of the Aga Khan Development Network (AKDN), the Aga Khan Foundation (AKF), seeks "to improve the quality of basic education by a programme of grants to governments and NGOs." Four objectives set the wider agenda of the Aga Khan Foundation: "Ensuring better early caring and learning environments for young children; increasing access to education; keeping children in school longer; and raising levels of academic achievement. In common with other donor agencies, the Foundation intends that girls and the very poor and geographically remote populations should receive special attention." The Aga Khan Program for Islamic Architecture (AKPIA) outlined elsewhere in this book is yet another example of the investments made in education by the Aga Khan, in this case in the context of existing institutions. By specifically targeting leading American institutions, and postgraduate learning in particular, the Aga Khan has not only insured the existence of excellent curricula focusing on the art and architecture of Islam, but, in so doing, he has laid the seeds for more than one generation of new scholars who have already gone on to enrich the discipline in the United States and many Muslim countries.

Although the scale and scope of these programmes already surpasses that undertaken by any other individual in the world, the Aga Khan is also at the origin of two significant universities. The first of these, the Aga Khan University (AKU), based in Karachi, provides post-graduate training of health service professionals, teachers and managers of schools, and encourages the work of research scholars. It was granted its charter in 1983 as Pakistan's first private, autonomous university. The twenty-six-hectare site of the Aga Khan University has undergone continual improvements and enlargements since the original complex was completed in 1985 and a new master plan calls for significant construction on the site in the years to come. With its focus on medical training the Aga Khan University is shortly to expand greatly on a second 200-hectare site, also near Karachi. The Faculty of Arts and Sciences (FAS) of the Aga Khan University is planned as nothing less than a reflection of the campuses of such universities as Yale and Harvard, ultimately a similar physical size. Finally, and also on a very large scale, the University of Central Asia (UCA) is planned for three large, entirely new campuses in Tekeli, Kazakhstan; Naryn, Kyrgyzstan; and Khorog, Tajikistan. The remote, mountain sites for these new facilities bring challenges to the architects and builders and substantial opportunities for populations that have been in good part cut off from higher education. Undertaken in collaboration with the governments concerned, the University of Central Asia is to be a non-denominational institution, underlining the fact that the Aga Khan has continually stressed pluralism and rejected sectarian exclusivity in his generosity.

What role does architecture play in all of this? The Aga Khan Program for Islamic Architecture of course emphasizes the history and development of architecture in the Muslim world, but when he has built, the Aga Khan has always placed great importance on the quality of the environments he creates. Thus, he has worked for more than thirty-five years with Tom Payette of Payette Associates on various aspects of the Aga Khan University in Karachi. He has given responsibility for the new University of Central Asia campuses to Arata Isozaki, one of the best-known architects in the world, insisting at every step of the way that students here and in the other institutions he has created should benefit from the comfort and quality of space that is essential to learning. It seems apparent that the Aga Khan believes that good architecture is a key part of learning and indeed of social interaction. In the same speech quoted at the beginning of this text, the Aga Khan stated: "Muslims believe in an all-encompassing unit of man and nature. To them, there is no fundamental division between the spiritual and the material, while the whole world, whether it be the earth, sea or air, or the living creatures that inhabit them, is an expression of God's creation. The aesthetics of the environment we build and the quality of the social interactions that take place within those environments reverberate on our spiritual life..."[2]

1 His Highness the Aga Khan, on receiving the Thomas Jefferson Foundation Medal in Architecture, University of Virginia, Charlottesville, Virginia, 13 April 1984.
2 Ibid.

Aga Khan University

KARACHI, PAKISTAN

Architect: Payette Associates, Boston

Date: design 1972–73; completed 1985;
                    additions 1990s–

■ The Aga Khan University and Teaching Hospital in Karachi is a seminal project in the development of the projects of the Aga Khan. The complex consists of a 721-bed teaching hospital, a medical school for 500 students, a school of nursing and housing for staff and students, all built on a twenty-six-hectare site donated by the government of Pakistan located just outside the city. Designed in 1972–73, the complex was completed in 1985. Selected after an international consultation, the architects, Payette Associates from Boston, well-known specialists in hospital design, visited numerous significant historic Islamic monuments in Spain, North Africa, Iran and Pakistan before undertaking their task. As they say: "Based on this research, a multi-layered set of guidelines was established for the physical layout, architectural development, landscape and interior design of the facility, based on local culture, climate and the specific attributes of the site." Interconnected by courtyards that almost make the identification of individual buildings difficult, the complex has been highly successful, both in professional and in architectural terms. Monumental portals lined in pink marble and often inscribed with verses from the Koran identify the points of entry to the major sections of the University. Traditional methods of passive climate control, such as terracotta *brise-soleils*, sloped roofs with wind scoops and thick walls provide relief from high temperatures and make the campus something of an oasis in the midst of an otherwise rather chaotic environment. This impression is heightened by the use of filtered light, water and vegetation in patterns that clearly recall Islamic tradition without ever approaching pastiche. The reinforced-concrete and concrete block buildings are rendered in "weeping plaster, a naturally pigmented cement plaster with a hue that is easy on the eye in the intense sun and which reduces glare by casting its own shadow."[1] Terracotta or teak screens, or marble wainscoting where people come into contact with exterior walls contribute to an overall feeling of user comfort.

An aerial view of the Stadium Road Campus of the Aga Khan University, Karachi, Pakistan.

A ramp in the Faculty of Health Sciences, in the Aga Khan University, Karachi, Pakistan.

The initial complex included about 93,000 square metres of floor area, and Payette designed an expansion of the teaching facilities of the School of Nursing in 1995, and an addition to the Radiology Department including an MRI unit in 1996. Community Health Services and Research buildings and a Sports and Rehabilitation Centre were completed shortly thereafter. The architects undertook a further master plan design beginning in 1999 with designs for an Ambulatory Care building, Cardiac Services, women's residence complex, Clinical Laboratory and an Oncology building. The site plans for the planned expansions show that the architects have carefully conserved the original pattern of open courtyards and spatial transitions while rendering the overall density somewhat greater. Some 3419 students graduated from the University in 2003, the largest number with a General Nursing (RN) Diploma. The institution had a full-time staff of over 4000 people the same year, including 447 full-time faculty members. When it is considered that Pakistan did not have similar facilities when this project was undertaken, the impact of the Aga Khan University in Karachi can begin to be measured. As the architect Tom Payette points out, the facilities can be compared in their size and nature to such prestigious institutions as the John Hopkins Medical School in the United States.

The Faculty of Arts and Sciences

Architect: Payette Associates, Boston

Date: construction 2009–

■ Having worked with Payette Associates for thirty-five years, the Aga Khan has recently undertaken another project with them in Karachi. The Faculty of Arts and Sciences (FAS) of the Aga Khan University is to be built on a 227-hectare site set fifty kilometres from central Karachi in an area designated by the government as "Education City". A further 200 hectares have been set aside for residential, campus-related areas, commercial space and the development of affiliated research institutes. The first phase of the design calls for 126,000 gross square metres of floor area for approximately 1600 undergraduates, which is to say as many as Harvard College. Indeed, the comparison to Harvard or Yale is not a vain one since the FAS complex, presently scheduled for phased construction between 2009 and 2015 with an opening in October 2012, will ultimately, which is to say in a more distant future period, be as large as the core area of the two prestigious American universities. Indeed, Payette Associates have worked on campus planning (beginning in 1977) and construction for Harvard and for numerous other universities including Yale. As was the case in the earlier work, Payette has carefully studied the Faculty of Arts and Sciences in terms of the comfort of users. They write: "The metaphor of a city in the desert elicits the articulation of several landscape typologies or zones that form a continuum of experience as one moves through the campus. Starting with the

A plan showing the proposed disposition of student housing on the future Faculty of Arts and Sciences Campus of the Aga Khan University in Karachi.

FACULTY OF ARTS AND SCIENCES | AGA KHAN UNIVERSITY

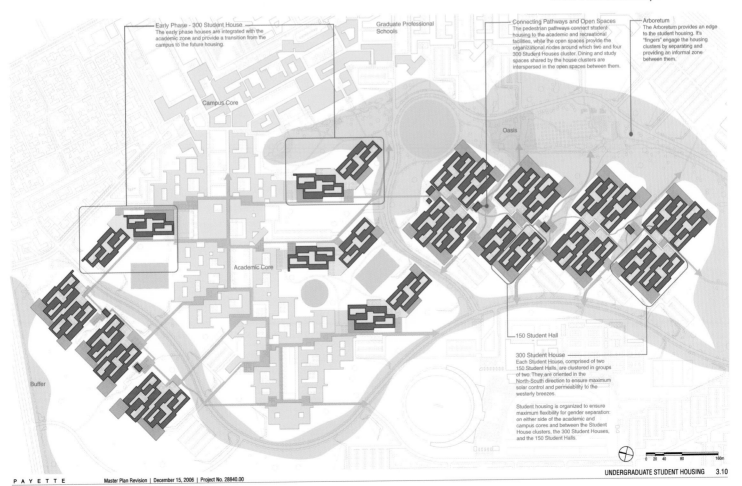

A plan by Payette Associates showing the proposed development of the new Faculty of Arts and Sciences of the Aga Khan University in Karachi, Pakistan.

natural desert condition, which supports a variety of plant growth, a transition landscape is introduced between building complexes and the desert. This transition landscape, described by Roberto Burle Marx as the 'middle landscape,' will assume an organized, designed character while maintaining visual consistency with the natural landscape. Elements of architecture – low walls, embankments, paths – will be found within this transition landscape, along with shade-loving groundcover and shrubs not otherwise found in the natural landscape to provide colour, texture and pleasant aromas in areas where people are passing or gathering. At points of entry into the various building complexes, a *bustan* is introduced to signify transition from the middle landscape to the highly designed and organized landscapes within the complex, manifested by courtyards and the major connecting pathways. Within the building complex, the integration of natural and building landscape with architecture will find its highest expression in lush, highly-designed courtyards that integrate hardscape, softscape, plantings and water."[2] Payette Associates are presently slated to design the buildings of the FAS complex. The ongoing relationship between the Aga Khan and Tom Payette has developed into one of the most interesting client-architect pairs in contemporary architecture. The natural modesty and professional integrity of Payette have produced not only buildings, but whole campuses that correspond to local conditions and also, in a profound way, to the humane and generous ambitions of the Aga Khan.

1 Payette Associates, *An Evolution of Ideas*, Melbourne 2003.
2 Payette Associates, Z07_0117_FAS_MasterPlan.

1   Campus Development

1A Academic Core

1B Graduate Professional Schools

1C Faculty/Staff Housing

    1C1 Senior Faculty and Administration Housing

1D Undergraduate Houses

1F Athletics

    1F1 Inter-collegiate Sports Center

    1F2 Informal Play Area

    1F3 Core-Campus Athletics

1G Infrastructure

    1G1 Warehouses and Offices

    1G2 Power Plant

    1G3 Chiller Plant

    1G4 Water Treatment

    1G5 Wastewater Treatment

    1G6 Solid waste handling

    1G7 Sludge drying beds

    1G8 Compost yard

    1G9 Communication tower

1H Site

    1H1 Main Campus Gate

    1H2 Service Gate

    1H3 Oasis

    1H4 Arboretum

    1H5 Stormwater Management System

    1H6 Buffer Zone

2   Off-Campus Development

2A Local retail-commercial District (8.9 Ha)

    2A1 Shops, restaurants, movies, etc.

    2A2 Hotel (250 rooms) & Conference Center

    2A3 Taxi stand, Jitney buses for AKU development

    2A4 Transportation stop

2B Multi-Story high density housing (9.5 ha, 1700 units)

2C High density single-family housing (14 ha, 840 units)

2D Medium density single-family housing (30 ha, 1000 units)

2E Low density single-family housing (100 ha, 1500 units)

2F Elementary School (2.8 ha)

2G Park

2H1 Senior Faculty and Administration Housing

2H2 Graduate and Married Student Housing (1200 Apt Units)

2H3 Graduate student sport center

3   Research Park (43 Ha, 210,000 GSM)

Additional ± 500 acres

Existing 560 acre AKU

University of Central Asia

TEKELI, KAZAKHSTAN
KHOROG, TAJIKISTAN
NARYN, KYRGYZSTAN

Architect: Arata Isozaki & Associates
Date: 2006–

■ The University of Central Asia (UCA) is one of the broadest and most unexpected of the education initiatives of His Highness the Aga Khan. Three campuses are currently planned: in Tekeli, Kazakhstan; Naryn, Kyrgyzstan; and Khorog, Tajikistan. One particularity of these remote sites is that they are located in the mountains. Both the Naryn and Khorog sites are over 2000 metres above sea level. The three campuses are being designed for approximately 1000 students and 200 faculty members each, with a planned floor area of about 100,000 square metres per location. As the official presentation of the project has it, the University of Central Asia has "a clear and focused goal: to foster economic and social development in the broad mountain regions of

Central Asia and elsewhere, while at the same time helping peoples to preserve and promote their cultural heritages." UCA will offer three main programmes, an undergraduate section leading to a Bachelor's degree in liberal arts and sciences, a post-graduate School of Development, offering a Master of Arts degree "in multiple areas that define the lives of mountain peoples," and a School of Continuing Education offering non-degree courses in local languages to mid-career professionals, civil servants, businessmen and women, and leaders of civil society organizations. It will also offer programmes for older learners and the general public in practical areas relevant to economic and social development.

The founders of the University of Central Asia are President Nursultan Nazarbayev of Kazakhstan, President Emomali Rakhmonov of Tajikistan, President Askar Akayev of Kyrgyzstan and His Highness the Aga Khan. In 1997 an International Commission was formed to plan the University, and in 2000 the International Treaty establishing the University was signed by the founders and subsequently ratified by the parliaments of Kazakhstan, Tajikistan and Kyrgyzstan. The Charter of the University

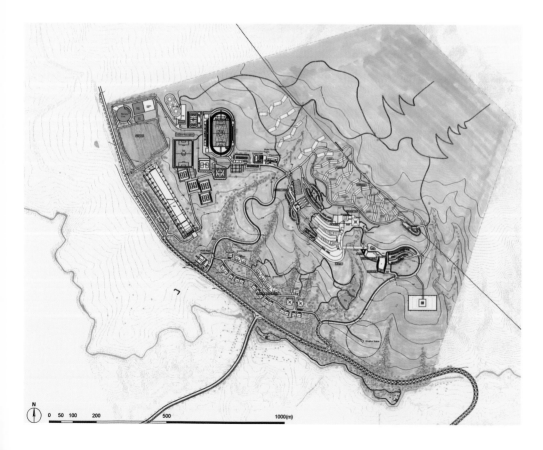

The campus of the future University of Central Asia in Tekeli, Kazakhstan, is located on a hilly, prairie site at an altitude of 1273 metres. It is thirty-five minutes east of the regional capital, Taldy-Korgan, and three hours by car from Almaty. Tekeli is at the mouth of the narrow valley along the Kazak steppe in the historic Zhedysu or Seven Rivers region. It borders the Alatau and Dzhungaria mountain ranges, with the Altai Mountains further north.

N 0 50 100   200   500   1000(m)

Khorog is the capital of the Badakhshan Autonomous Region of Tajikistan. It is located in the heart of the Pamir or "Roof of the World" Mountains, near Afghanistan, northern Pakistan and south-west Xinjiang in the People's Republic of China. The campus site, known locally as Dasht, is a prominently elevated triangular terrace at an altitude of 2080 metres, just north-west of the town centre.

of Central Asia explicitly affirms that the UCA is a secular institution of higher education espousing no religion or creed and open to men and women of all faiths and traditions, or with no religious beliefs, purely on the basis of merit. Preliminary site work was carried out by Sasaki Associates of Watertown, Massachusetts. The architect for all three new campuses, selected in 2004, is Arata Isozaki, one of the most noted Japanese creators. Born in Oita City on the Island of Kyushu in 1931, Arata Isozaki graduated from the Architectural Faculty of the University of Tokyo in 1954 and established Arata Isozaki & Associates in 1963, having worked in the office of Kenzo Tange. Winner of the 1986 RIBA Gold Medal, his notable buildings include: the Museum of Modern Art, Gunma (1971–74); the Tsukuba Centre Building, Tsukuba (1978–83); the Museum of Contemporary Art, Los Angeles (1981–86); Art Tower Mito, Mito (1986–90); the Centre for Japanese Art and Technology, Cracow, Poland (1991–94); Higashi Shizuoka Plaza Cultural Com-

plex, Shizuoka; and Ohio's Centre of Science and Industry (COSI), Columbus, Ohio. More recently, aside from the Yamaguchi Centre for Arts and Media, Yamaguchi, Japan (2001–03), he was called on to design a number of projects in Qatar, including the National Library and the master plan for the Qatar Education City. He is currently completing the Shenzhen Cultural Centre, Shenzen, China (1997–2005/).

Arata Isozaki, who met the Aga Khan when he was a member of the 1998 Master Jury for the Award, had never been to Central Asia before receiving this commission, although he does currently have extensive work in China, for example. The task of construction in these remote mountain locations is complex, with winter lasting as much as eight months. The risk of seismic activity on the sites further complicates design. Topographic surveys for the locations were carried out by the London engineering firm Arup. Isozaki explains that each site is different – Tekeli on a prairie with hills, Khorog on a plateau

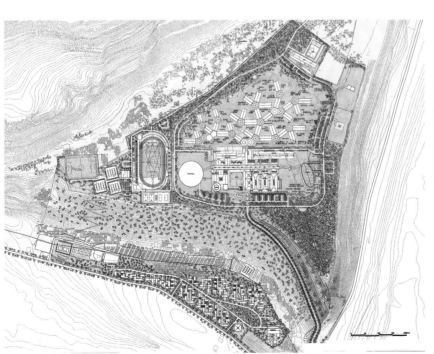

and Naryn in a mountain valley. Each of the campuses will have a tower, a ceremonial courtyard and a colonnade. Nazeer Ladhani, President of the University of Central Asia explains: "The idea is that each campus should reflect its own environment and topography, but there has to be something in common on the three campuses to signify the unity of the institution. There are certain common design features like the tower or the pre-eminent libraries. The layout is influenced by the surroundings, but the components are very similar – student life, academic buildings and residences and so on."[1] The plans for Tekeli are based on triangular designs, Khorog on rectangular or square forms and Naryn on round shapes. Khorog will place an emphasis on dark stone cladding with open-joint walls, copper eaves and such traditional local finishes as stucco. Thus each campus will have its particularities and rely to the greatest extent possible on local materials and traditional methods. Arata Isozaki compares the construction of these new universities to that of medieval monasteries in the mountains, albeit with much more modern methods and designs. Isozaki is certainly interested in the challenge of using "basic natural elements and construction," an idea, he points out, that is quite popular today among China's young architects.[2]

Clearly, the goals of the new university are ambitious: "The University of Central Asia will give the approximately forty million men and women from Central Asia's mountain regions an alternative, and draw promising talent from elsewhere to the challenges of economic and social development in mountain regions. It will provide mountain peoples with the skills necessary to generate income for themselves and their families and to create new jobs. It will give them greater leverage in their growing interactions with the down-country economic centres. It will provide skills and develop leadership that will enable mountain peoples to participate fully in the modern world. It will also help enable them to preserve and at the same time to benefit from the environment of which they are the guardians."[3]

1 Interview with Nazeer Ladhani, Geneva, Switzerland, 29 June 2006.
2 Interview with Arata Isozaki, Gouvieux, France, 19 December 2006.
3 University of Central Asia (UCA).pdf, at: http://www.akdn.org.

Naryn province or *oblast* is in the Tien-Shan mountain range of Kyrgyzstan. Its capital, Naryn, is four hours by car from the Kyrgyz capital of Bishkek and an equal distance from Kashgar in the People's Republic of China. Ak-Kya, the UCA campus site, stretches along a bend of the Naryn River, twelve kilometres downstream from the city at an altitude of 2050 metres.

Aga Khan Academies

VARIOUS LOCATIONS WORLDWIDE

Architects: Mombasa Academy, Kenya: Farouk
Noormohamed Design Associates,
Vancouver, Canada, with Planning
Systems Services, Nairobi, Kenya
Dar es Salaam Academy, Tanzania: still to
be selected
Hyderabad Academy, India: HCP Design
and Project Management Private Limited
(HCP), India

Dates: Mombasa Academy: completed 2003
Dar es Salaam Academy: 2005–
Hyderabad Academy: 2006–

Education must also make the case for a pluralistic tradition in which other views, ethnicities, religions and perspectives are valued not only because that is just and good, but also because pluralism is the climate best suited for creativity, curiosity and inquiry to thrive. It must also stimulate students to consider a variety of perspectives on some of the fundamental questions posed by the human condition: 'What is truth?' 'What is reality?' and 'What are my duties to my fellow man, to my country and to God?' At the same time, education must reinforce the foundations of identity in such a way as to reinvigorate and strengthen them so that they can withstand the shock of change.[1]

His Highness the Aga Khan

■ In 2000, the Aga Khan created a programme for the creation of an integrated network of schools, called Aga Khan Academies, "dedicated to expanding access to education of an international standard of excellence. The Academies, which will educate young men and women from pre-primary through higher secondary education, are planned for key locations in Africa and Asia." The Aga Khan Education Services already operates 300 schools in Pakistan, India, Bangladesh, Kenya, the Kyrgyz Republic, Uganda, Tanzania and Tajikistan with some 54,000 students enrolled in classes ranging from preschool to higher secondary education. This system, though greatly expanded by the present Aga Khan, was created by his grandfather, Sir Sultan Mohamed Shah, Aga Khan III. Two hundred schools were established in the first half of the twentieth century, the first of them in 1905 in Zanzibar, Gwadur, Pakistan and Mundra, India. Other schools are presently envisaged in Afghanistan, the Democratic Republic of the Congo, Madagascar, Mali, Mozambique and Syria.

The first Aga Khan Academy opened in August 2003 on a new 7.3-hectare campus in the Kizingo area of Mombasa, Kenya. The project architect was Planning Systems Services of Nairobi, with FNDA (Vancouver) as consulting design architect. As the Aga Khan stated at the inauguration of the school: "The buildings and spaces of a school, often the first exposure of young people to architecture and designed spaces, both edu-

Left, an aerial view of the Aga Khan Academy campus in the Kinzingo area of Mombasa, Kenya.

Right, admission to the Aga Khan Academies is 'means-blind', that is, selection is based not on the ability to pay, but on academic strengths and the overall potential of the students.

cate the eye of students and reinforce the intellectual standards and cultural rootedness of the institution. The comments of parents about the architecture of the school at Kilindini illustrate gratifyingly their awareness of the connection between the intellectual and physical standards of a school."[2]

President Mkapa of Tanzania and the Aga Khan laid the foundation stone of a second Aga Khan Academy in Dar es Salaam on 17 March 2005. A similar ceremony took place in Hyderabad, India, on 22 September 2006, when the Aga Khan and the Chief Minister of Andra Pradesh, Dr Y. S. Rajasekhara Reddy, launched work on a forty-five-hectare site allocated by the government of the state in 2005. The principles and guidelines for the campus were established in this instance in collaboration with the American planners Sasaki Associates from Watertown, Massachusetts. HCP Design and Project Management Private Limited (HCP) of India have been selected as architects for the Academy. Well-known in India, HCP has completed more than 800 projects in the country. As the Hyderabad complex is described: "The buildings and spaces of the Academy will seek to provide an aesthetically well-conceived environment conducive to reflection, to study and enjoyment within an appropriate cultural context. Early construction will include the Academy Building, which will be the functional heart of the campus, housing not only the books, technology, computer labs, seminar rooms, library staff and study space of the Senior school but the offices of admissions and administration. The Academy Building will also house the Professional Development Centre (PDC), which will develop the Academy's own teachers as well as teachers from other schools, both private and government." Eleven other Aga Khan Academies are planned for the Democratic Republic of the Congo, Madagascar, Mali, Mozambique, Uganda, Bangladesh, Pakistan, Afghanistan, the Kyrgyz Republic, Tajikistan and Syria.

1 His Highness the Aga Khan, quoted in: academies.Brochureinternational.pdf, at: http://www.akdn.org/academies/index.htm.
2 Speech by His Highness the Aga Khan at the inauguration ceremony of the Aga Khan Academy Kilindini, Mombasa, Kenya, Saturday 20 December 2003.

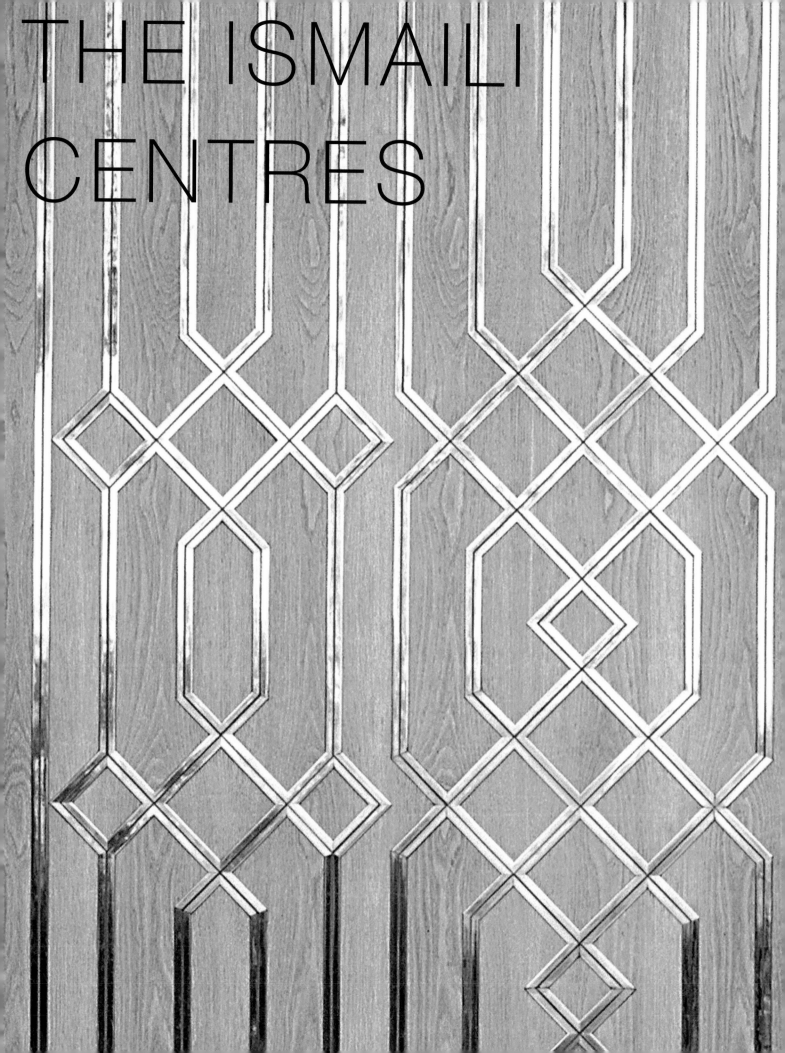

THE ISMAILI
CENTRES

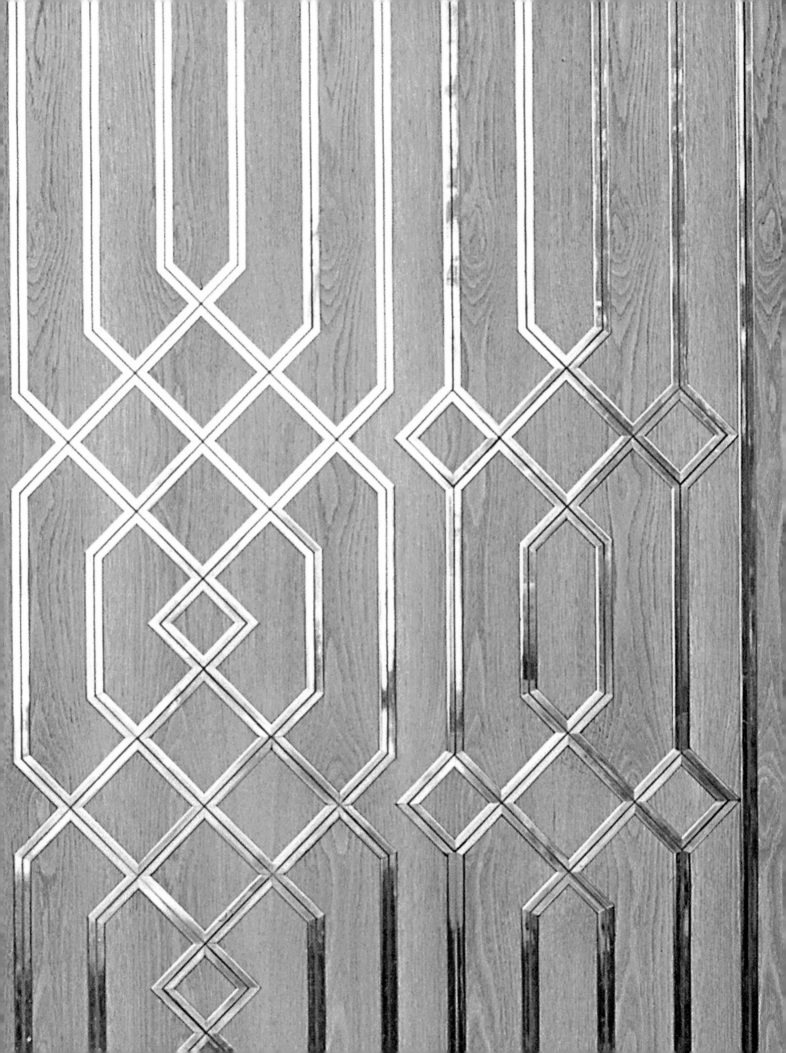

The Ismaili Centres

We have clarity and direction enough when the Koran affirms that to save a life is, as if, to save humankind altogether. It is in this context that I request that you view the Ismaili Jamatkhana and Centre, Houston, as much, much more than a place of congregation and a home for administrative offices. The Centre will be a place of peace, humility, reflection and prayer. It will be a place of search and enlightenment, not of anger and of obscurantism. It will be a centre which will seek to bond men and women of this pluralist country to replace their fragility in their narrow spheres by the strength of civilized society bound together by a common destiny.[1]

His Highness the Aga Khan

The Aga Khan has done a great deal to make people across the world aware of the issues facing architecture in the Muslim world. Through educational institutions, his sponsorship of the Aga Khan Award for Architecture and work on the ground by the Aga Khan Historic Cities Programme he has created a now indispensable link between the past, the present and the future of architecture in parts of the world often ignored or underestimated in the West. There is a strong and present relation between this extensive involvement in architecture and the religious responsibilities of the Aga Khan. He stated in 1984: "As the Imam of a twelve-million strong community spread among some twenty-five countries, I have been constantly concerned with the construction of schools, clinics, hospitals, office complexes and indeed ordinary housing. In so doing I have become more and more concerned with the physical form that the Islamic world of the future will take and with how technological experience can be appropriately utilized to assist it … My awareness that there might be a case for seeking to reinvigorate and perhaps reorient the built environment of the Islamic world was awakened by the needs of my own Ismaili community. But I decided very early on that to attempt to tackle my own constituency alone could be interpreted as self-serving and might even isolate us from other Muslims if they did not genuinely share our concerns. The problem appeared generic to the whole Islamic world and if this was confirmed, as indeed it was, it had to be approached in the widest context."[2]

The Ismaili Centre in Houston is one of a growing number of such buildings erected in London, Burnaby in Canada, Lisbon, Toronto, Dubai, and Dushanbe in Tajikistan. All of these centres are places of prayer and gathering for the Ismaili community in the countries concerned. Indeed, it is the very history of the community that has placed a particularly great responsibility on the shoulders of the Aga Khan. He explains: "In 1957, I was still a student at Harvard when I inherited the responsibilities of the Ismaili Imamat from my grandfather, Sir Sultan Mohamed Shah. It seemed inconceivable then that there would ever be substantial communities in the West. The Ismailis were too deeply rooted in their ancestral homes, indeed frozen there by the Cold War in Asia, the Middle East and Africa. But dislocations in the wake of decolonialization, and more recently the collapse of the Soviet Union and the prolonged difficulties in Afghanistan have caused a number of Ismailis to seek new lands and homes. These migratory movements over the last half century have resulted in a substantial Ismaili presence in Russia, in Western Europe, the United Kingdom and Portugal, and particularly in the United States and Canada."[3]

The Ismaili Centres thus far created have often been the work of non-Muslim architects like Hugh Casson (London), Bruno Freschi (Burnaby) and Raj Rewal (Lisbon). The architects have worked nonetheless with briefs that call for "a synthesis of Islamic architecture and contemporary building design, a synthesis of architectural principles steeped in the tradition of the Faith, while at the same time coexisting with the requirements of modern-day society – a fusion symbolic of the Ismaili community." Often quite physically substantial, as in the case of the 18,000-square-metre facility in Lisbon, the Ismaili Centres have thus far not necessarily broken new ground in contemporary architecture in any conventional sense. They have represented solid and surely lasting efforts to create bridges between the past and the present, and above all between Islam and such significant locations as the Cromwell Road in London. They have also provided strong symbols and comfort for the Ismaili diaspora. The quality of the architecture of the Ismaili Centres is undeniable, however architecture needs to be understood in these cases in terms of the broader objectives enunciated by the Aga Khan himself: "A place of search and enlightenment, not of anger and of obscurantism," as he stated in Houston in 2002 in the wake of the events of 11 September 2001.

1 Speech by His Highness the Aga Khan at the inauguration of the Ismaili Centre and Jamatkhana, Houston, 23 June 2002. See: http://www.akdn.org/speeches/texas.html.
2 His Highness the Aga Khan, on receiving the Thomas Jefferson Foundation Medal in Architecture, University of Virginia, Charlottesville, Virginia, 13 April 1984.
3 Speech by His Highness the Aga Khan at the inauguration of the Ismaili Centre and Jamatkhana, Houston, 23 June 2002. See: http://www.akdn.org/speeches/texas.html.

Ismaili Centre and Jamatkhana

LONDON, UNITED KINGDOM

Architect / Planner: Casson Conder Partnership

Date: 1981

■ The first 'high-profile' Ismaili Centre to be built in the West was designed by the London architects Casson Conder Partnership for a very visible site in South Kensington, on the Cromwell Road, opposite the Victoria and Albert Museum and diagonally across the street from the Museum of Natural History. A religious, social and cultural meeting place, the building contains a Prayer Hall, but also social spaces and a gallery. Sir Hugh Casson (1910–99) was director of architecture at the 1951 Festival of Britain on London's South Bank. Working with Neville Conder, Casson designed the Elephant House at the London Zoo and worked on the master planning of the Sidgwick Avenue arts faculty buildings at the University of Cambridge. Provost of the Royal College of Art (1970) then President of the Royal Academy (1976–84), he designed the interior of the royal yacht *Britannia* and was also credited with teaching Charles, Prince of Wales, to paint in watercolours. As a member of the first two Steering Committees for the Aga Khan Award for Architecture (1980, 1983) Hugh Casson had a significant influence on the creation and early directions of the Award.

Left, windows and panels are in stainless steel, teak and bevelled glass, with three different surface finishes for the granite.

Below, the roof garden with its central fountain and four radial water channels.

The London Ismaili Centre certainly holds a significant place in the history of the involvement of the Aga Khan in architecture. As His Highness stated when it was decided to build the Centre: "This building and the prominence of the place it has been given indicate the seriousness and the respect the West is beginning to accord Muslim civilization, of which the Ismaili community, though relatively small, is fully representative. May this understanding, so important for the future of the world, progress and flourish. I sincerely believe that when this Centre is completed, it will be, both by its presence and the function it fulfils, an important addition to the institutions in London, a source of pride to all who took part in its creation, and a pledge and token of understanding between East and West."[1]

The focal point of the building is the Prayer Hall located on the second floor, but for religious reasons, it cannot be photographed. The building also contains a smaller prayer hall, classrooms for religious instruction of

children, an office, a multi-purpose social hall and a separate art gallery and exhibition space. In 1951, a religious, cultural and social centre was created by the Ismaili community in Kensington Court in London, which moved, in 1957, to Palace Gate in the Borough of Kensington. A site for a new centre was selected in 1971 at Albany Street in the Borough of Camden. The present site was acquired thereafter and on 6 September 1979 Lord Soames, then Lord President of the Council, laid the foundation stone in the presence of the Aga Khan. At that time Lord Soames said that the new building would "remind Londoners that not all architecture sprang from Greek and Italian roots." The architects were asked to "respect the mood of Islamic architectural tradition" while fitting into an area that can only be described as heterogeneous but Western in terms of the inspiration of its buildings. Members of the Ismaili community, Islamic scholars and architects or designers specialized in Islamic design were consulted as part of the process of Casson Conder. Also of importance was the capacity of the building to receive a relatively large number of people without upsetting the routines of the community, and to provide a quiet environment within despite the hustle and bustle of the urban setting. The top floor of the building provides for an unusual garden, designed by Don Olson of Sasaki Associates. The use of running water, a play of light and shade and an integration of interior and exterior spaces are part of the aspects of this area that fully respect Islamic tradition while maintaining a modern feeling. A comprehensive attempt was made in the interiors to reconcile the "aesthetics of traditional Islamic interior design with an aesthetic that was at the same time contemporary and situated in a Western context." Decorative patterns link the exteriors and interiors of the building. The use of stylized and abstract calligraphy, honeycombing (*muqarnas*) and carved woodwork (*mashrabiyya*) are part of the efforts of the architects to create the stated link between the Muslim world and the West. Essentially, this link is at the very heart of the project of the Aga Khan in erecting an Ismaili Centre in such a prominent location in London.

1 His Highness the Aga Khan, in: *The Ismaili Centre*, London 1985.

Right, in an inversion of the more common order, the granite cladding on the upper part of the volume is relatively closed, while windows below, in this night view, make the lower part of the building glow from within.

Below, the main stairway of the Centre with its large chandelier.

180

Left, the social hall, and, below, the council chamber in the Imaili Centre, London, United Kingdom.

Right, the Brazilian blue granite fountain pool in the entrance hall is set on an interweaving geometric floor pattern intended to be "characteristic of Islamic art."

Ismaili Centre and Jamatkhana

BURNABY, BRITISH COLUMBIA, CANADA

Architect / Planner: Bruno Freschi
Date: 1984

It will be a place of congregation, of order, of peace, of prayer, of hope, of humility and brotherhood. From it should come forth those thoughts, those sentiments, those attitudes which bind men together, which unite. It has been conceived and will exist in a mood of friendship, courtesy and harmony. It is my hope that it will become a symbol of growing understanding in the West of a very deep and real meaning of Islam.[1]

His Highness the Aga Khan

■ Located in a "tree-lined suburb of Greater Vancouver," the Burnaby Centre was the first purpose-built structure of its kind in Canada. Ismailis first arrived in Canada in the mid 1960s, mostly as students. The population increased with political upheavals in East and Central Africa and in particular the expulsion of Asians from Uganda by Idi Amin in 1972. The Ismaili National Council for Canada is based in Vancouver, whence the desire to build a centre there. The architect of the Centre, Bruno Freschi, was born in Trail, Canada, in 1937. He studied in London at the AA (Architectural Association) before joining the firm of Arthur Erickson (Massey-Erickson, Vancouver) in 1964. He was the chief architect and planner of the 1986 Vancouver Exposition site. Although of Italian Catholic background, he took on the Burnaby commission with a sense of the importance of the work he was carrying out, building a bridge between two worlds in many senses.

The design brief, once again, required that the building be "a synthesis of Islamic architecture and contemporary building design, a synthesis of architectural principles steeped in the tradition of the Faith, while at the same time coexisting with the requirements of modern-day society – a fusion symbolic of the Ismaili community." As is the case in London, the focal point of the building is the Prayer Hall, "emphasizing its primary religious function providing facilities for prayer." The building also serves as the administrative headquarters for the Ismaili community and includes a social hall, administrative offices, a council chamber and classrooms. Built in warm beige sandstone, based on a double-square plan and including six octagonal stairwells in the corners, the geometric, octagonal theme is repeated in interior decors as are calligraphic themes inspired by the traditions of Islam. Sandblasted coral and rose marble panels inlaid with brass are used to form the *mirhab*, in the Muslim architectural indication of the direction of prayer. Thirteen octagonal domes with brass circle rings bring natural light into the space. The building is acceded to through a courtyard garden containing fountains, trees and flowers. An ivory-coloured marble portal marks the main entrance. The building is centred on a 1.5-hectare site and aligned on an east-west axis. Five copper domes and glazed cupolas mark the roof of the building. The description of the building affirms that "the building is a fusion of timeless aesthetic principles of a functional facility and an environment to sustain the sacred purpose to which it is dedicated. In Islam, man is answerable to God for whatever man creates, and this is reflected in Islam's architectural heritage."[2]

1 His Highness the Aga Khan, foundation ceremony of the Ismaili Centre and Jamatkhana, Burnaby, Canada, 26 July 1982.
2 *The Ismaili Jamatkhana and Centre*, Burnaby, B.C., Canada 1985.

Below, the west facade of the Burnaby Ismaili Centre is clad in Carrara marble and Italian sandstone.

Right, the opalescent cast-glass windows in the Prayer Hall are decorated with stained geometric patterns.

Ismaili Centre and Jamatkhana

LISBON, PORTUGAL

Architect / Planner: Raj Rewal; Frederico Valsassina
Date: 1998

Dedicated to the preservation of spiritual values, the promotion of social development and the enhancement of intellectual discovery, the Ismaili Centre will seek to contribute to the enjoyment by citizens of Lisbon, and visitors alike, of spaces and buildings whose inspiration will aim to empathize as well as expand our cultural horizons.[1]

His Highness the Aga Khan

■ After the Burnaby and London Ismaili Centres, the Lisbon building was the first such facility in continental Europe. The first Ismailis arrived in Portugal in the mid 1960s. As was the case in Canada, upheavals in Eastern and Central Africa in the 1970s led many Ismailis to settle in Portugal. An Ismaili National Council was created in the country in 1979 and the Aga Khan Development Network has been active in the country since 1983. Working with such partners as the Gulbenkian Foundation and the University of Minho, the AKDN has been actively expanding its efforts to better educational and social conditions for underprivileged children in Portugal. Five architects were invited to present schemes for the Lisbon Ismaili Centre and the winner was Raj Rewal, born in 1934 in India. His built work includes the Nehru Pavilion, Scope office complex, Central Institute of Educational Technology, World Bank building, National Institute of Immunology, Parliamentary Library, and the Asian Games Village, all located in New Delhi. A professor at the New Delhi School of Architecture and Planning, he has placed great emphasis on the importance of affordable housing. He was a member of the 2001 Master Jury of the Aga Khan Award for Architecture. In Lisbon, he worked with the local architect Frederico Valsassina who designed the Eden Theatre and the Olympic Swimming Pool in the city.

The site of the Lisbon Ismaili Centre covers no less than 18,000 square metres, of which 9825 square metres is covered by construction (including 1935 square metres for courtyards). This leaves a large landscaped area of 12,200 square metres. The building is quite large because it includes not only a Prayer Hall, but community and multi-purpose areas as well as offices for the Aga Khan Foundation, the Ismaili Institutional Council and teaching facilities. The sources of inspiration listed by the architect are numerous and include Lisbon's Monastery of the Hieronymites (1502–52) designed in the Manueline style by Diogo Boitac, India's Fatehpur Sikri and Spain's Alhambra. In India, Rewal used computer-driven stone cutting techniques for his World Bank and Parliamentary Library projects. Here, early in the process, careful studies were made of the engineering aspects of the building in consultation with Peter Rice. Rewal's rather heavy latticework design, constituted in good part of granite and steel with limestone cladding in some places, is certainly original and calls on numerous aspects of Islamic design, including recurring geometric patterns. The structural stonework lattice had to take into account that Lisbon is in an earthquake zone. Domes are suspended on pre-stressed cables. A main courtyard is laid out in the tradition of the Islamic garden with water channels, flowering plants and a central fountain. The protected calm found here is intended to close out the surrounding, busy urban environment and provide a place of peace and contemplation. Indeed, this is the architect's response to the lofty goal set by the Aga Khan in this case: "To achieve equilibrium between human existence and the Absolute, and therefore to attend to both spiritual and physical needs."

1 His Highness the Aga Khan, foundation ceremony of the Ismaili Centre and Jamatkhana, Lisbon, Portugal, 18 December 1996.

Right, the central courtyard of the Lisbon Ismaili Centre with its fountain and *chahar-bagh*-style garden.

For the Lisbon Ismaili Centre, the architect sought inspiration from a wide variety of sources including Persian gardens, the Alhambra, Fatehpur Sikri and, more unexpectedly, Lisbon's Monastery of the Hieronymites.

Ismaili Centre and Jamatkhana

DUSHANBE, TAJIKISTAN

Architect: Farouk Noormohamed Design Associates
                  (FNDA), Vancouver, Canada
Date: 2003–

The recent history of this entire region has been one of considerable change and turmoil. Fortunately, wisdom has prevailed, ushering in a period of peace, reconstruction and renewal, rendering even more tolerant, more open and more inclusive, a valued heritage. It is my earnest hope that the creation of the Ismaili Centre in Dushanbe will contribute to this endeavour. Its design will draw inspiration from the magnificent landscapes of this region, but also from its architecture, construction techniques, materials and decorative traditions. In seeking to enliven the encounter of the past with the future and foster a mutually rewarding dialogue between tradition and modernity, the Centre will attempt to reflect lessons from structures both monumental and mundane, from spaces both religious and social. The Centre will seek to provide a place where people will come together to share their creativity and their wisdom. Above all, it will be a place for contemplation, upliftment and the search for spiritual enlightenment.[1]

His Highness the Aga Khan

■ Dushanbe is the capital of Tajikistan, a mountainous, landlocked country in Central Asia that borders on Afghanistan to the south, Uzbekistan to the west, Kyrgyzstan to the north and China to the east. It has one of the lowest per capita GDPs among the fifteen former Soviet republics. It was estimated in 2003 that the country has a population that is eighty-five per cent Sunni Muslim and five per cent Shia Muslim. Dushanbe, a small town until about eighty years ago, had a population of about 562,000 people at the moment of the 2000 census. Khorog, in Tajikistan, is one of the three sites selected for the University of Central Asia presently being designed by the Japanese architect Arata Isozaki. The Ismaili Centre announced for Dushanbe in 2003 is the first such facility to be located in Central Asia.

The architects of the Dushanbe Ismaili Centre are Farouk Noormohamed Design Associates (FNDA) based in Vancouver, Canada. Founded in 1986, the firm has done a considerable amount of work for the Ismaili community, including *jamatkhanas* in Markham, Ontario, Burnaby Lake, Atlanta, north London, Los Angeles, Dallas and future facilities in Calgary and Edmonton, as well as a number of projects at the Aga Khan University in Karachi (with Payette Associates). The architect specifically describes the architecture in terms of both local and Ismaili traditions: "The essence of the design concept is derived from the Persian garden. First, the Garden of Eternity consists of four rivers: Wine, Milk, Honey and Clear Water." Working with the Vancouver landscape architect Fred Liu and Associates, Noormohamad states: "One of the essential responsibilities of a landscape architect is to take the elements of nature, together with the man-made elements and combine both to arrive at an elegant scheme." "The five towers," he goes on to explain, "remind the believer of the Panjtan Pak – reminiscent of the five pillars used in the construction of the traditional Pamiri house. But here, the interpretation of these pillars reminds the Ismaili that whereas in the past the five pillars within their home reminded them of their faith and the challenges to practising their *tariqah*, here, in a new political and social climate, the five towers, serving as symbolic pillars, now hold up the endless sky as the roof – and reassure the believer that now the entire world is his home. It represents a symbolic connection with the *umma* and the *jamat* worldwide, all of whom share the same roof, held up by the same pillars and beliefs." In terms more specifically related to the architecture, Farouk Noormohamed evokes the entrance portal of the complex: "Once through this portal, the magnificent great court becomes visible, its strong sense of geometry and symmetry unmistakably Islamic, and its look and feel modern but clearly rooted in the Central Asian idiom. Here, he is greeted by bubbling fountains and large open spaces ideal for gathering in good weather and for public events such as Eid prayers. The four-*iwan* layout is reminiscent of the great courtyards of

Drawings and plan of the new Dushanbe Ismaili Centre show that it is a substantial structure, inspired both by local tradition and, in a larger way, by Islamic architecture. The large, symmetrical square inner court and garden, with its central fountain, is clearly visible in the plan.

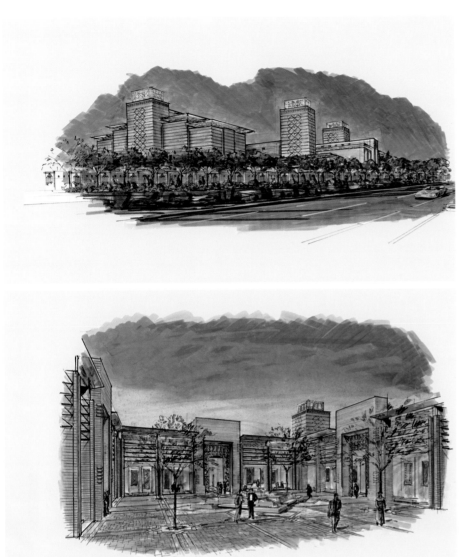

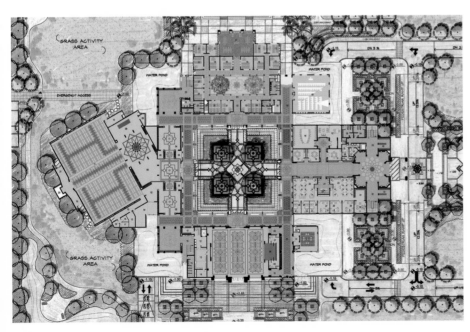

Samarkand, Bukhara and Khiva and places a very local context to an otherwise very modern structure. The opening in the wall leading to the youth and education courtyard reveals a space markedly different from the gallery space. Its residential scale provides a place of comfort and a nurturing environment for its primary users – the youth. The linear courtyard leads to smaller courtyards to give the younger children attending classes direct access to outdoor spaces adjacent to their classrooms. These courtyards also lead to outdoor play areas and a performance amphitheatre where performing arts and dance, such an integral part of Tajik culture, can be explored in an outdoor setting … Looking toward the courtyard, and above, glass louvers provide shading of the walkways and are treated with sandblasted calligraphy which, when lit from the side, will appear as though floating in mid air."

Throughout, the spirit of tolerance and openness expressed by the Aga Khan is the leitmotif of this building. Energy efficiency and "ecologically benign materials" are used, while "the building form and plan are integrated with the site, the region and the climate to increase and encourage a harmonious relationship between the inhabitants and nature for the surrounding community." The architect has also paid careful attention to the potential for seismic activity in the region, creating an "elastic roof diaphragm" designed to transfer the stress engendered by an earthquake to the supporting elements of the structure.

1 Address by His Highness the Aga Khan at the foundation stone ceremony of the Ismaili Centre, Dushanbe, Tajikistan, 30 August 2003. See: http://www.akdn.org/speeches/15_dushanbelC.htm.

Ismaili Centre and Jamatkhana

DUBAI, UNITED ARAB EMIRATES

Architect: Rami El Dahan & Soheir Farid RDSF

Date: 2004–07

The transformation of the small trading port that was once Dubai into a vibrant metropolis has paralleled its demographic growth and cosmopolitan evolution. The intermingling of cultures that so enlivens this thriving city is one of the strengths on which Dubai has built its renown as a point of global convergence. It is precisely this notion of convergence that has characterized the Ismaili community's successful endeavours to contribute, through the institutional framework of the Aga Khan Development Network, toward addressing critical development challenges of the day. The Centre will provide facilities to promote cultural, educational and social programmes from the broadest, non-denominational perspectives within the ethical framework of Islam. Amongst them will be an Early Learning Centre where the Aga Khan Education Services, a philanthropic agency, will draw on its own extensive experience in many parts of the world to offer broad, holistic, early childhood education on a secular and non-denominational basis at the highest international standards of excellence. The objective is to have a curriculum of proven calibre, taught by competent teachers, to help lay strong foundations for a child's continuing educational growth.[1]

His Highness the Aga Khan

■ In a trend shown in a number of his speeches in the early twenty-first century, the Aga Khan here addresses not only the pivotal role of Dubai in its region, but also the nature of the work that he expects this new Ismaili Centre to undertake. He makes a deliberate connection between the situation of the world and the place that his institutions can or should occupy. The Dubai Centre is clearly intended as an ambitious link between Ismailis, but also in a broader and more ecumenical sense between Muslims and the rest of the world. Continuing the description of the Centre's role and its relation to Muslim tradition in his 2003 speech, the Aga Khan stated: "At this juncture, perhaps, it would be appropriate to situate one of the functions of the Ismaili Centre in the tradition of Muslim piety. For many centuries, a prominent feature of the Muslim religious landscape has been the variety of spaces of gathering coexisting harmoniously with the *masjid*, which in itself has accommodated a range of diverse institutional spaces for educational, social and reflective purposes. Historically serving communities of different interpretations and spiritual affiliations, these spaces have retained their cultural nomenclatures and characteristics, from *ribat* and *zawiyya* to *khanaqa* and *jamatkhana*. The congregational space incorporated within the Ismaili Centre belongs to the historic category of *jamatkhana*, an institutional category that also serves a number of sister Sunni and Shia communities, in their respective contexts, in many parts of the world. Here, it will be space reserved for traditions and practices specific to the Shia Ismaili *tariqah* of Islam."[2]

At a time when Dubai is undergoing one of the most substantial architectural revolutions of any city in

In a decided contrast with the towers of Dubai, the new Ismaili Centre calls on Fatimid tradition for the inspiration of its forms. The Egyptian architects Dahan and Farid had used similar formal sources in their Hilltop Restaurant in Azhar Park, Cairo, Egypt.

192

the world, recently completing the tallest skyscraper on earth, the Aga Khan has chosen not to create an Ismaili Centre in this spirit of astonishing modernity, but rather looks back in some sense to the sources of Muslim tradition. "In the tradition of Muslim spaces of gathering," he says, "the Ismaili Centre will be a symbol of the confluence between the spiritual and the secular in Islam. Architect El Dahan has drawn inspiration from the Fatimid mosques in Cairo. Like its functions, the Centre's architecture will reflect our perception of daily life whose rhythm weaves the body and the soul, man and nature into a seamless unity. Guided by the ethic of whatever we do, see and hear, and the quality of our social interactions, which resonate on our faith and bear on our spiritual lives, the Centre will seek to create, inshallah, a sense of equilibrium, stability and tranquility."[3]

Muslims represent ninety-six per cent of the population of the United Arab Emirates, with Shia Muslims numbering about sixteen per cent of the total. Dubai is the most populous of the seven Emirates and quite unusual in that expatriates, roughly 100,000 British and other Westerners, as well as significant numbers of Indians or other nationalities, constitute a good part of its population. Although Sunni Islam is the religion of state, Dubai in particular allows substantial freedom of worship. Shia mosques, for example, are considered private and receive no government funding. Dubai is also the only Emirate that has Hindu temples and a Sikh *gurdwara*.

The architects of the new Centre are the Egyptians Rami El Dahan and Soheir Farid (El Dahan & Farid Ltd.), who designed the Hilltop Restaurant, inspired by Fatimid and Mamluk building traditions, in Azhar Park in Cairo. Here, again, Rami El Dahan has openly called on Fatimid traditions. Knowledge of Fatimid designs is limited by the fact that there are only five mosques from the period left in Cairo – al-Azhar, al-Hakim, al-Aqmar, al-Saleh Talai and the small mosque of al-Juyushi on the plateau of the Muqattam overlooking the city. As the architect describes the building: "The project has many courtyards and water features which are important elements in the architecture of the Islamic world; the courtyards range in size and scale from the intimate Morning Prayer Hall courtyard with its *salsabil* to the large courtyard with the large fountain and a *chahar-bagh* garden." Rami El Dahan goes on to explain: "We also have seven main feature domes in the project with genuine designs, notably the sixteen-metre-span Congregation Hall dome carried on eight intersected arches, forming an octagonal star, the dome of the Morning Prayer Hall, a multi-facet prismatic brick dome, carried over large intersected stone vaults

and the dome of the heptagonal hall with seven sides." As is the case with other major Ismaili Centres, the Dubai facility is quite substantial (15,500 square metres of floor area). The main Prayer Hall alone covers 1342 square metres and a total of more than 7000 square metres is used for courtyards and gardens. The first Ismaili Centre and Jamatkhana to be located in the Middle East, the Dubai Centre has a basement, ground level and three storeys above ground and is built on a 13,200-square-metre site given by His Highness Sheikh Mohammed bin Rashid Al Maktoum to His Highness the Aga Khan.

With its accomplished wood and stonework, the Centre bears a clear relation to the past, as its architects wished. It gives the feeling of a building intended to last, like monuments of other eras. In the midst of the real-estate boom that has swept over Dubai, the Ismaili Centre recalls the traditions of a region more than of this specific location. In this cosmopolitan, expatriate-dominated city on the Gulf, the Ismaili Centre is a signal that the lessons of the past still have meaning today. In its Prayer Hall, before the stone *mirhab* wall, but also under its brick domes, the Centre materializes a sense of spirituality that cannot be captured in photography.

1 Speech by His Highness the Aga Khan at the foundation stone-laying ceremony of the Ismaili Centre and Jamatkhana in Dubai, United Arab Emirates,13 December 2003.
2 Ibid.
3 Ibid.

Below, a plan showing the ways in which the architects have integrated the complex plan for the Dubai Ismaili Centre into this corner site.

Right, the Congregation Hall dome with its clear reminiscences of Islamic architecture of the past.

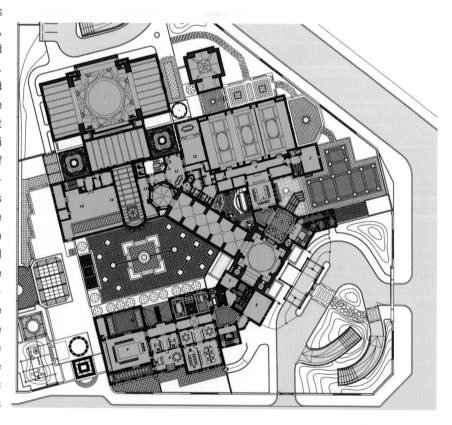

THE CHALLENGE
OF PLURALISM:
PROJECTS
IN CANADA

The Challenge of Pluralism: Projects in Canada

There are approximately 75,000 Ismailis in Canada, of whom 15,000 reside in the Greater Vancouver area. The first of these citizens arrived in the mid 1960s, often as students from such countries as India, Pakistan or Bangladesh (West Pakistan until 1971). The flow of Ismailis toward Canada, a country long-known for its tolerance and acceptance of the ideas of pluralism, increased in the 1970s due to conflicts in Africa and in particular the expulsion of Asians from Uganda in 1972. Though some come from Zaire, South Africa, Rwanda, Iran and Syria, a majority of Canadian Ismailis originated in Kenya, Uganda, Zanzibar and Tanzania. It was no coincidence that the first Ismaili Centre and Jamatkhana to be built in North America was opened in Burnaby, Vancouver, in 1984, not long after the London Centre was inaugurated.

Today, the Aga Khan has undertaken to give his presence and that of his community in Canada an even more significant and symbolic turn. Two major projects in Ottawa and two in Toronto have clearly marked these initiatives. Given the importance that the Aga Khan has long placed on architecture, it should be noted that the responsibility for three of these projects has been given to two of the best-known contemporary architects in the world, Fumihiko Maki from Japan and Charles Correa from India. The fact that neither of these architects is a Muslim might be seen as a further pledge to the principles of pluralism that have come to underlie the Canadian initiatives of the Aga Khan. Maki has designed the Delegation of the Ismaili Imamat in Ottawa as well as the new Aga Khan Museum in Toronto, while Correa is the architect selected to create a second Canadian Ismaili Centre, on the same Wynford Drive site in Toronto as the Museum. Both architects, as well as the landscape designer Vladimir Djurovic from Beirut, have been actively encouraged, not only by the programmatic requirements laid out for them, but in more personal terms by the Aga Khan himself, to seek to renew the principles of the architecture of Islam in a contemporary vocabulary and in full respect for the context they are working in. When he announced the Toronto buildings in 2002, the Aga Khan stated: "In situating these two institutions in Canada, we acknowledge both a tradition of tolerance and inclusiveness as well as an environment that has permitted diversity to flourish, enriching the civic life of each individual and community that has sought to make this country its home. It is to this commitment to pluralism that we will turn in seeking to make these institutions both a repository of heritage and a source of inspiration for societies the world over in the future."[1]

The original announcement for the Aga Khan Museum in Toronto carried with it the prospect for a centre for the study of "human pluralism." As it happens, that project has also taken form, but in a different location, the former Canadian War Museum on Sussex Drive in Ottawa. In announcing this project, the Aga Khan stated: "I am grateful that the government of Canada has contributed so generously to its material and intellectual resources. Making available the Old War Museum is a particularly generous and symbolic gesture. Our own commitment is to invest in this building so that it becomes a worthy testament to Canada's global leadership in the cause of pluralism. Those who talk about an inevitable 'clash of civilizations' can point today to an accumulating array of symptoms which sometimes seems to reflect their diagnosis. I believe, however, that this diagnosis is wrong –

that its symptoms are more dramatic than they are representative – and that these symptoms are rooted in human ignorance rather than human character. The problem of ignorance is a problem that can be addressed. Perhaps it can even be ameliorated – but only if we go to work on our educational tasks with sustained energy, creativity and intelligence. That is why we felt the Global Centre for Pluralism was needed. That is why the Global Centre for Pluralism exists today. And that is why the Global Centre for Pluralism holds such enormous promise for all of our tomorrows."[2]

Built beginning in 1904 to plans by the firm Band, Burritt, Meredith and Ewart, the 3800-square-metre structure selected for the Pluralism Centre has a clear importance for Canadians since it housed the Dominion Archives until 1967 and the War Museum, until a new structure was created on another site in 2005. Indeed, in contrasting the crystalline elegance of Maki's new design for the Imamat Delegation building and this old stone structure that is soon to be refurbished (architect still to be selected), it may be possible to further sense the deeper meaning of the involvement of the Aga Khan in architecture. In a letter sent to Fumihiko Maki to detail the wishes of the Aga Khan for the building, in 2002, it was written: "The Imamat Delegation building, in a sense, should be somewhat mysterious and visually nearly esoteric. It should not be blatant, but ethereal: not obvious, but difficult to captivate; it should be harmonious, linear in many planes and shapes, at times symmetrical and sometimes asymmetrical, perhaps domed in some areas with spherical or flat planes…"[3] The will thus expressed had to do not only with the functions of the new building, but also with the neighbouring buildings in Ottawa. Architecture is seen here not as a simple container, prestigious or attractive as it may be; rather, it is the real use of a building, how it fits into its context, what message it gives through the flow of light and the rising forms of a remarkable glazed atrium that interests the Aga Khan.

Housing the Dominion Archives for most of the twentieth century, the older building on Sussex Drive, later chronicling the history of Canada's wars, could not be better and more symbolically suited to the Global Pluralism Centre imagined by the Aga Khan. The diversity inscribed in the country's population, the ravages of war, both these powerful forces mark the Ottawa building and give it legitimacy to become a forum, in the very core of the nation, to reach out to those who would doubt the virtues of understanding and tolerance. The Islam defended by the Aga Khan speaks with the voices of pluralism, of the very diversity at the heart of a religion that spans the globe. The four new projects in Canada, one steeped in local history, the other three reaching pointedly to a future where modernity respects tradition and even improves upon it, are all a statement for the significance of architecture as a vehicle for ideas, as points of gathering where people may meet and learn to be tolerant of one another.

1 Speech by His Highness the Aga Khan, Toronto, Canada, 8 October 2002.
2 Remarks by His Highness the Aga Khan on the occasion of the signing of the funding agreement for the Global Centre for Pluralism, Ottawa, Canada, 25 October 2006.
3 Letter from Nizar Shariff to Fumihiko Maki, 10 October 2002.

Delegation of the Ismaili Imamat

OTTAWA, CANADA

Design Architect: Fumihiko Maki & Maki and Associates, Tokyo, Japan

Architect of Record: Moriyama & Teshima Architects, Toronto, Canada

Date: 2004–08

One of the most prominent features of the Delegation of the Ismaili Imamat in Ottawa, Canada, is its glass-covered atrium. The asymmetrical form of this crystalline emergence was the result of a close dialogue between the architect and the Aga Khan.

■ The Delegation of the Ismaili Imamat in Ottawa is located at 199 Sussex Drive on a site measuring approximately one hectare. The building borders on many of Canada's prominent diplomatic and political sites, such as Parliament Hill, the official residences of the Governor General and the Prime Minister, as well as numerous embassies and consulates. This stretch of Sussex Drive is also called Confederation Boulevard, a ceremonial thoroughfare in the nation's capital. The building will, for all intents and purposes, function much like an embassy. "It will be an enabling venue for fruitful public engagements, information services and educational programmes, all backed by high-quality research to sustain a vibrant intellectual centre and a key policy forming institution," according to the Aga Khan. "The aim," he continues, "will be to foster policy and legislation that enables pluralism to take root in all spheres of modern life: justice, the arts, media, financial services, health and education."

Designed by the noted Japanese architect Fumihiko Maki, the two-storey building, due to be completed in 2008, will have a gross area of 8916 square metres, of which 4720 above grade. The primary spaces of the Centre are a reception and exhibition gallery, library, conference and meeting rooms, institutional offices, a boardroom and executive office, as well as residential space. Born in Tokyo in 1928, Fumihiko Maki received his Bachelor of Architecture degree from the University of Tokyo in 1952, and Master of Architecture degrees from the Cranbrook Academy of Art (1953) and the Harvard Graduate School of Design (1954). He worked for Skidmore, Owings & Merrill in New York (1954–55) and Sert Jackson and Associates in Cambridge, Massachusetts (1955–58), before creating his own firm, Maki and Associates, in Tokyo in 1965. Fumihiko Maki was the winner of the 1993 Pritzker Prize, the Prince of Wales Prize (for Hillside Terrace) and the UIA Gold Medal the same year.

He received the Praemium Imperiale, given by the Japan Art Association, in 1998. He was also a member of the 1986 and 1992 Master Juries for the Aga Khan Award for Architecture. Given his American educational background and cosmopolitan manner, Fumihiko Maki has received numerous commissions in North America, including the Centre for the Arts in the Yerba Buena Gardens (San Francisco, California, 1993) and the Sam Fox School of Design and Visual Arts at Washington University in St Louis (2006). Aside from the Aga Khan Museum in Toronto and the Delegation of the Ismaili Imamat published here, he is currently advancing on the University of Pennsylvania Annenberg Public Policy Centre (2008), the Media Arts and Sciences Building at MIT (2009), and a skyscraper in lower Manhattan (World

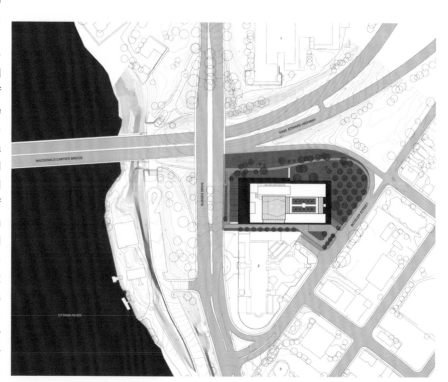

Trade Centre Tower 4, 2012). Fumihiko Maki is also working on numerous projects in Japan.

The site of the building is irregular with elevation changes of as much as four metres. The western side of the property is on Sussex Drive, where architectural guidelines are set by Canada's National Capital Commission. A residential neighbourhood on the east and a roadway with the Ottawa River beyond on the west contrast with the south boundary formed by the fences of the Embassy of the Kingdom of Saudi Arabia. Set on a granite podium that helps to deal with the changes in elevation on the site, the building offers numerous plazas and terraces. As Maki states: "Together with the space planning, the podium helps to achieve an intended ambiguous division between indoor and outdoors spaces – an inherent characteristic found in much of Islamic architecture."

Working in close collaboration with the Aga Khan, Professor Maki has developed an asymmetrical, crystalline form for the main atrium of the building. As the architect says: "Contained within a simple rectilinear footprint (43.5 metres wide and 87 metres long), the plan form is shaped in the configuration of an elongated 'ring' whereby the programmes surround two large symbolic

Given the constraints imposed by the harsh winter climate of Ottawa, Fumihiko Maki chose not to use running water in the garden courtyard of the Delegation building (lower right). Elsewhere, his light, subtle touch is evident in these perspective drawings.

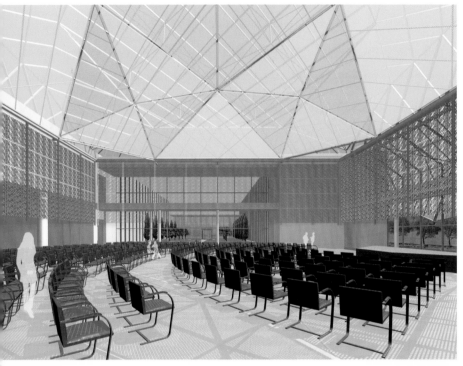

spaces that are complimentary – an atrium and court-yard. The building as a whole will be an interplay of visual clarity and opacity, overlaid with various degrees of translucency. Like the natural beauty of a rock crystal that is a true wonder to the human eye, it is hoped that the Delegation building will be a source of optimism, fascination and enlightenment." The idea of light and the play on contrasting opacity or transparency is a constant theme of this work. "The building is clad primarily in glass with varying degrees of transparency, translucency and opacity to achieve a dynamic visual effect. The primary facades on Sussex Drive and Boteler Street are affixed with crystallized glass panels – Neoparies. It is a unique building material developed and made by a highly sophisticated and specialized technique of crystallizing glass whereby the process produces needle-shaped crystals to give the glass a soft opaque colour resulting in a smooth marble-like texture. Neoparies is no doubt a product of our modern age; however, it evokes a sense of continuity and tradition with the masonry buildings nearby. The north and south elevations are arranged in alternating bands of transparent and translucent glass which is hoped will achieve different levels of visual penetration into the building as well as subtle reflections of the surrounding landscape."

The atrium is set to the west and accessible from the ceremonial entrance on Sussex Drive, while an outdoor garden "recalling the traditional Persian-Islamic garden – the *chahar-bagh* (a garden contained within walls that is divided into four quarters by the intersection of four avenues)" is near the eastern Boteler Street entrance. The architect explains that these two spaces form the building's hub linking the different parts of the programme and creating an "inner sanctuary somewhat separated from the outside world." Fumihiko Maki states: "His Highness the Aga Khan is a strong advocate and supporter of pluralistic values. These are thought to be expanded through academic, governmental and cultural exchanges. In architecture, this concept can be expressed through themes such as modernity versus tradition, West versus East. The design of the Delegation building is a manifestation of this vision held by the Aga Khan carried out with the principles of modernism that also reflect an Islamic character in its spatial and detail design."

Ismaili Centre and Jamatkhana

TORONTO, CANADA

Design Architect: Charles Correa Associates
Architect of Record: Moriyama & Teshima Architects
Date: 2006–

■ The new Ismaili Centre and Jamatkhana in Toronto, located on the same Wynford Drive site as the Aga Khan Museum, will contain a library and conference rooms for the community, administrative offices and chambers for the Ismaili Council for Canada, as well as the Social Hall for gatherings, lectures, seminars and other special occasions. Located at the highest point of the site, the entrance portico faces the driveway and on the garden side the building opens onto terraces overlooking the Don Valley. The total floor area of the Ismaili Centre and Jamatkhana is 7800 square metres, with construction due to begin in 2007. Together with the Aga Khan Museum, the new Ismaili Centre and their surrounding gardens offer an oasis of calm and serenity to an area that is presently in need of such an amenity.

In 2000, the architect Charles Correa won an international competition to design the Toronto Ismaili Centre and Jamatkhana. His built work includes the Mahatma Gandhi Memorial at the Sabarmati Ashram in Ahmedabad, the Jawahar Kala Kendra in Jaipur and the State Assembly for Madhya Pradesh. He has completed housing projects in Delhi, Bombay, Ahmedabad and Bangalore. He was Chief Architect for the "Navi Mumbai", a new city for two million people located across the harbour from Bombay. He was appointed by Prime Minister Rajiv Gandhi as the first Chairman of the National Commission on Urbanization. He has been serving recently as the Farwell Bernis Professor in the School of Architecture and Planning at MIT. He was the 1994 recipient of the Praemium Imperiale in Japan, as well as winner of the RIBA Gold Medal in 1984 and the UIA Gold Medal in 1990. He has been one of the most consistent participants in the activities of the Aga Khan Award for Architecture in various capacities from the time the Award was first created. He was a member of the 1980, 1983, 1986, 2001 and 2004 Award Steering Committees, and of the 1989 Award Master Jury. He received an Aga Khan Award in 1998 as the architect of Vidhan Bhavan (Bhopal, India), the State Assembly for the government of Madhya Pradesh, completed in 1996.

Left, gardens designed by Vladimir Djurovic will accompany the Centre as well as the Museum.

Above right, a large crystalline dome is a prominent feature of Charles Correa's design for the Toronto Ismaili Centre.

Below right, an overall site plan shows the Centre to the left and the future Aga Khan Museum by Fumihiko Maki to the right.

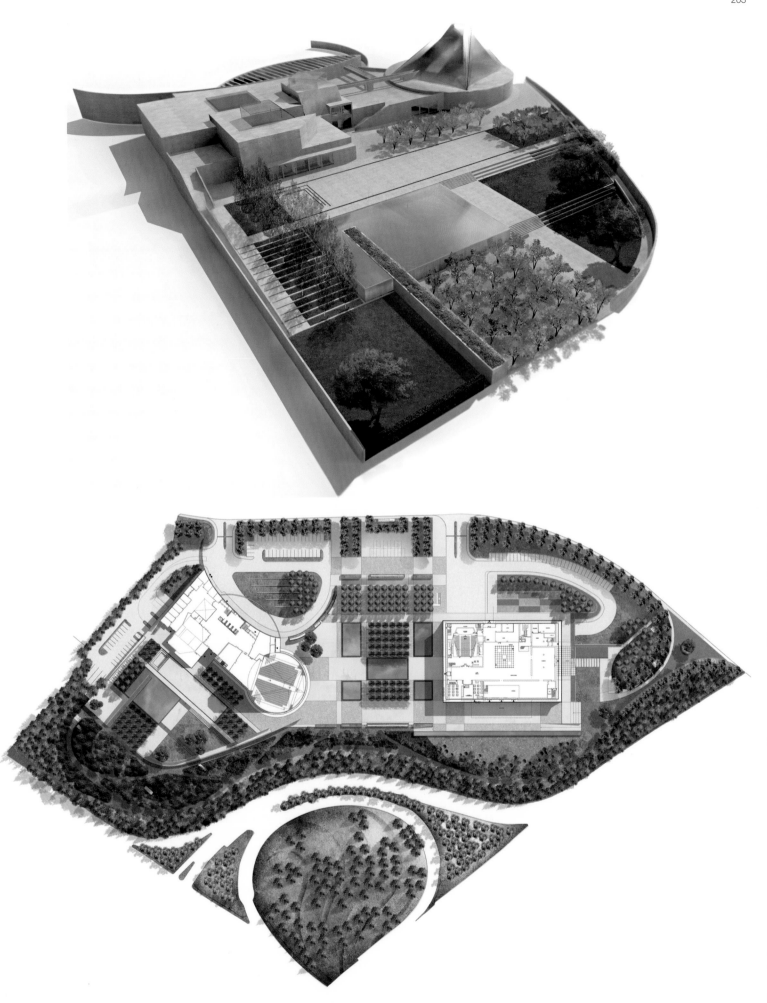

Below, drawings by the office of Charles Correa show the Prayer Hall and dome of the Toronto Ismaili Centre.

Right, the Centre as seen in a computer perspective by the landscape designer Vladimir Djurovic.

The generous double-height Social Hall of the Centre has its own entrance foyer, contiguous with that of the Prayer Hall, allowing for a good deal of flexibility in the use of the spaces. The Social Hall opens out toward the "Ismaili Garden" designed by Vladimir Djurovic (see page 212). The library is contained in the double-height atrium, a space that connects with the administrative offices and Council Chamber above.

The climax of the composition is the Prayer Hall. Approaching it from the entrance foyer, a glass column symbolizing the unity of Islam is visible. The actual Prayer Hall is circular in form, "like a gigantic tent, with light cascading down from the immense vault of the sky above."[1] Although the round form might be considered quite unusual, Charles Correa thus sees it as a reference to the connection of religion to history and the majesty of creation. For the roof, the architect has used two layers of frosted glass that enclose a delicate steel fabric, modulating light in the space. While the exterior of the Prayer Hall roof is made up of varying flat surfaces, the architect compares the interior surfaces to the facets of a diamond or the forms generated by fractal geometry. The result is "a rational and contemporary reinvention of the age-old Islamic tradition of corbelling." Clearly visible from the Don Valley Parkway, at night this roof will "glow from within like a jewel,"[2] becoming the most powerfully symbolic architectural gesture of the complex.

Charles Correa explains: "We knew this Jamatkhana must be pluralistic – expressing on the one hand the age-old heritage of the Ismaili community, and on the other their newfound aspirations as proud citizens of Canada. So, throughout the building, the architectonic language and the materials used are contemporary (exposed concrete, stainless steel and frosted glass), but there are also references to other values, derived from other times. Thus, for instance, though the orientation of the building has been determined by its immediate surroundings, as we move toward the Prayer Hall, the axis pivots in order to face Mecca. This subtle but dramatic shift (clearly articulated in the floor plans and sections) serves to remind us that underlying the pragmatic world of our everyday lives, there exists a more sacred – and profound – geometry."[3]

1 E-mail from Charles Correa, 20 February 2007.
2 Ibid.
3 Ibid.

Aga Khan Museum

TORONTO, CANADA

Design Architect:	Fumihiko Maki & Maki and Associates, Tokyo, Japan
Architect of Record:	Moriyama & Teshima Architects, Toronto, Canada
Date:	2006–

■ As described in a report from Toronto's Commissioner for Economic Development, Culture and Tourism: "On 8 October 2002, the Aga Khan Development Network (AKDN) announced its intention to establish in Toronto a museum housing exceptional collections of Islamic art and heritage items, as well as a cultural and educational centre devoted to the study and practice of human pluralism. The location for this proposed development is a seven-hectare site located on Wynford Drive in the north-west quadrant of Don Valley Parkway and Eglinton Avenue. The site includes a 3.6-hectare parcel upon which the Aga Khan Development Network had previously proposed constructing a mosque, and an adjacent 3.35-hectare parcel that the Aga Khan Development Network has recently acquired from Bata Industries." In its conclusion, the report states: "The Aga Khan Development Network proposal would appear to be a major acquisition for the City of Toronto and demonstrates that the world recognizes Toronto's long-standing tradition of tolerance. It further adds to Toronto's appeal as a vibrant international city capable of competing for prominent business, research and cultural attractions. This announcement made world coverage in many major newspapers increasing Toronto's worldwide profile."[1]

After the original site planning done by Don Olsen of Sasaki Associates, the architects Charles Correa (Ismaili Centre and Jamatkhana) and Fumihiko Maki (Aga Khan Museum) became involved in the project on adjacent parcels. The Aga Khan Museum is intended as a "multi-purpose cultural facility with the aim of exhibiting Islamic art and artefacts, providing a venue for musical performances, educating the general public on Islamic traditions, along with a full service restaurant. The programme consists of four primary functions (museum, auditorium, educational and multi-purpose) organized around a central courtyard."

Early in the development of the Wynford Drive site, the Aga Khan wrote a letter to Fumihiko Maki outlining some of his ideas for the facility: "For the Aga Khan Mu-

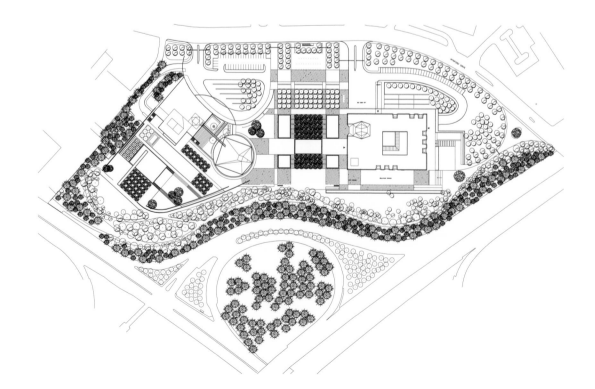

Left, on the site plan, the Aga Khan Museum is visible to the right, with its essentially rectilinear plan.

Right, models show the relation of the Museum to Correa's Ismaili Centre on their shared Wynford Drive site in Toronto, Canada.

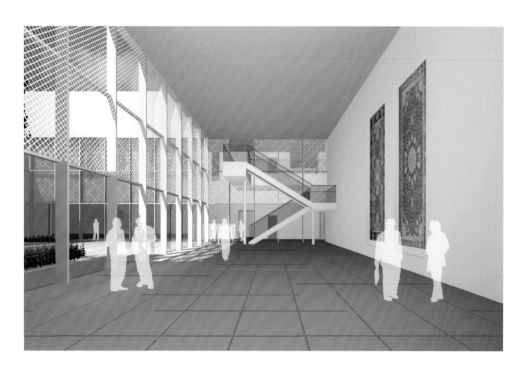

Although these perspectives do not yet give the layman a clear understanding of the Museum's volumes, it is clear that, as imagined by the architect, the building will be flooded with light wherever the conservation of the displayed art works permits.

seum, I thought that 'Light' might be a concept around which you could design an outstanding museum; the notion of Light has traversed nearly all of human history and has been an inspiration for numerous faiths, going as far back of course as the Zoroastrians and their reverence for the Sun, to the Sura in the Holy Koran titled Nour. Decades of Western history are referred to as the 'Enlightenment' for good reason."[2] The letter of the Aga Khan clearly explains the relationship of the client to the architect in this instance, expressed in terms of the ephemeral but essential qualities of light. "I hope that the building and the spaces around it will be seen as a celebration of Light and the mysteries of Light, which nature and the human soul illustrate to us at every moment in our lives," states the Aga Khan. "I have explained at the beginning of this letter why I think Light would be an appropriate design direction for the new museum and this concept is of course particularly validated in Islamic texts and sciences: apart from the innumerable references in the Koran to Light in all its forms, in nature and in the human soul, the light of the skies, their sources and their meaning has for centuries been an area of intellectual inquiry and more specifically in the field of astronomy. Thus the architecture of the building would seek to express these multiple notions of Light, both natural and man-

made, through the most purposeful selection of internal and external construction materials, facets of elevations playing with each other through the reflectivity of natural or electric light, and to create light gain or light retention from external natural sources or man-made internal and external sources."[3]

The 11,000-square-metre building is to be laid out on three floors: two floors above grade and one below for parking or reserves. The two floors above grade are to contain 1800 square metres of gallery space, a multi-purpose auditorium, a restaurant, and educational spaces consisting of classrooms and a library. Fumihiko Maki states: "Contained within a simple rectilinear footprint, the four primary functions will revolve around a central courtyard, which will act as the heart of the building and will integrate the differing functions into a cohesive whole while allowing each space to maintain its independence, privacy and character."[4] The architect has been careful to create ideal conditions for the viewing of art, providing very low luminosity where miniatures from the collections of the late Prince Sadruddin Aga Khan might be shown, for example. Skylight screens with geometric patterns "inspired by the windows in mosques" and translucent marble walls will be features of the exhibition spaces. The design is centred around a courtyard intended as "a

symbolic space, protected from the outside world," with an "inherent link to traditional Islamic architecture." The exterior of the Museum is "inspired by the forms and shapes of precious stones" and will have walls inclined at two distinct angles to accentuate the play of light on the surfaces. Translucent marble and opaque white marble are the main cladding materials. As for the relation with Correa's Ismaili Centre, Fumihiko Maki states: "The metallic roof of the auditorium space will further accentuate the shape and materiality of a precious stone and is intended to establish a formal dialogue with the crystal roof of Correa's Prayer Hall adjacent to the Aga Khan Museum. The primary entrance and axis of the Museum is aligned with the Prayer Hall, which will provide a subtle relationship between the two buildings, emphasizing the unity of the complex."

Luis Monreal, the General Manager of the Aga Khan Trust for Culture, underlines the significance of the Museum in the present world situation: "The evolution of the political situation in the last few years, its resulting crises and the additional factor of flows of emigration toward the West, have revealed – often dramatically – the considerable lack of knowledge of the Muslim world in Western societies. This ignorance spans all aspects of Islam: its pluralism, the diversity of the interpretations of the Koranic faith, the chronological and geographical extension of its history and culture, as well as the ethnic, linguistic and social diversity of its peoples. The supposed 'shock of civilizations' is in reality nothing more than the manifestation of the mutual ignorance that exists between two long-time neighbouring worlds. For this reason, the idea of creating a museum of Muslim culture, as an eminently educational institution with the aim of informing the North American public as to the diversity and importance of Muslim civilization, naturally imposed itself in the Aga Khan Trust for Culture's programmes."[5]

1 Staff Report from Joe Halstead, Commissioner of Economic Development, Culture and Tourism to the Economic Development and Parks Committee of the City of Toronto, 20 November 2002.
2 Letter from His Highness the Aga Khan to Professor Fumihiko Maki, 3 January 2006.
3 Ibid.
4 Fumihiko Maki & Maki and Associates, internal report.
5 Luis Monreal, in: '"Splendours at Court"– A Preview of the Aga Khan Museum in Toronto', forthcoming.

Interior views from the office of Fumihiko Maki show the auditorium (below) and an exhibition space (right) of the Aga Khan Museum in Toronto, Canada.

Gardens of the Toronto Ismaili Centre and the Aga Khan Museum

TORONTO, CANADA

Architect: Vladimir Djurovic Landscape Architecture,
              Beirut, Lebanon
Date: 2006–

■ An international competition was held to select the landscape architect who would be given the task of uniting the Aga Khan Museum designed by Fumihiko Maki and the Toronto Ismaili Centre designed by Charles Correa on the seven-hectare site selected in Toronto for both institutions. The young Lebanese architect Vladimir Djurovic was selected from a group of accomplished landscape architects. Djurovic, a cosmopolitan figure who owes his name to his Yugoslav father, states the goals of his scheme in simple terms: "Our vision for the project is one that captures the essence of the Islamic garden and translates it into an expression that reflects its context and contemporary age. Embracing the five senses as the means to reach the soul, every space and every garden are imbued with the delicate sensations that we seem to have lost in this fast-paced era. The ephemeral and the eternal are both essential to our composition of spaces. Shadows, light, petals, leaves and water in motion are complemented by the solidity and purity of created forms. All is not at once apparent; the garden reveals itself slowly to the visitor, who experi-

ences hidden aspects with serendipity." Being the intermediary figure between two such well-known architects as Maki and Correa cannot be simple, but Djurovic has succeeded in creating "one unique, harmonious and welcoming park with two landmark buildings in it. The park," he says, "could be viewed as fluctuating between formal spaces around the buildings and informal spaces as one moves away."

Educated in the United Kingdom (Reading University) and in the United States (University of Georgia), Vladimir Djurovic created his own firm in Beirut in 1995 and has practised an intriguing mixture of minimalist architecture and landscape design since then, in particular for numerous private clients. He admits to being attracted to the craftsmanship of the Swiss master Peter Zumthor or the ways in which the Portuguese architect Eduardo Souto de Moura integrates his work into its natural settings. "After I won the competition," explains Vladimir Djurovic, "His Highness gave me a list of places to visit around the world. 'Once you have visited these places, let us meet again,' he said. I have never been to

Left, a garden view showing the Toronto Ismaili Centre at the rear of the perspective with the Aga Khan Museum on the left.

Right, images showing the proposals of the landscape architect for the gardens near the Centre.

India and I found the Gardens of Humayun's Tomb and Fatehpur Sikri remarkable."[1]

Built in honour of Sufi Saint Salim Chishti in 1571 by the Mughal Emperor Akbar, Fatehpur Sikri might be considered a revealing choice in the context of the itinerary of Vladimir Djurovic. Unlike other Mughal cities it demonstrates a certain informality and improvisation and blends influences from Hindu and Jain sources as well as Islamic elements. Further, Fatehpur Sikri is known to have influenced such modern figures as Charles and Ray Eames and Balkrishna Doshi. After visiting India, Djurovic finished his whirlwind tour in Azhar Park in Cairo. "I realized after these visits," says the landscape architect, "that what the Aga Khan is doing is not for now, it is for generations to come. I understood that anything I do for him has to last as long as possible."

The designs of Vladimir Djurovic for the 75,000-square-metre Toronto gardens are an intentional attempt to render contemporary the very spirit of the Islamic garden. "I think that His Highness is happiest when he discusses the gardens. He really wants us to reinterpret the Islamic garden in a contemporary way. We did not copy any garden – it is more about what you feel and smell and hear in an Islamic garden. What it is that I love about Alhambra is the sound of water and the smell of jasmine. I wanted to use a very contemporary language. The architecture of the buildings is very contemporary. The garden must also reflect its context as well – a place covered with snow. I like this challenge – how to reinterpret the Islamic garden."[2]

Such features as the waterfall 'bustan' (Arabic for "fruit garden"), a secluded yet welcoming space, is a niche in the botanical garden that serves as a gateway to the Ismaili Centre. One area of particular attention and concern in the frigid winter climate of Toronto was the use of water in the gardens. "In one preliminary scheme we created translucent cast acrylic elements with water flowing over the edges. Covered with snow, they would appear like lit ice cubes. The edges would have been angled out so that freezing ice falls off the edge of the basins," explains the designer. This idea was abandoned in favour of solid granite basin walls because Djurovic could not vouch for the long-term reliability of acrylic slabs, which tend to turn yellow with time. Within the newly designed granite basins, their edges still angled out to allow expanding ice to fall over the edges, Djurovic places what he calls "steel lilies" that create turbulence in the water when it is liquid, and are heated in winter to produce steam and the continuing sound of water in movement. A rose garden elsewhere uses the scents and origins of the varieties selected to give a subtle lesson to visitors about the geographic dispersion across the world of the Ismaili community.

Through his seductive but quite realistic computer perspectives, Vladimir Djurovic has conquered the enthusiasm of those involved in the Toronto projects, giving a sense of unity to what could have become a disparate whole, especially given the decidedly urban context of the site, with major traffic arteries located just beyond this green vision of paradise. Through sight, but also sound and smell, this Lebanese designer with a Yugoslav name recreates an Islamic garden in a land of snow, a garden of pluralism.

1 Interview with Vladimir Djurovic, Paris, France, 31 January 2007.
2 Ibid.

The gardens of Vladimir Djurovic are designed to give colour to the site in all seasons, as these four views from the same perspective demonstrate.